Art

for All – I
The Framework

Developing art in the curriculum with pupils with special educational needs

Melanie Peter

Advisory Teacher for the Arts Norfolk LEA

David Fulton Publishers

David Fulton Publishers Ltd
2 Barbon Close, London WC1N 3JX

First published in Great Britain by
David Fulton Publishers 1996

Copyright © Melanie Peter

British Library Cataloguing in Publication Data

A catalogue record for this book is available from the British Library

ISBN 1-85346-317-5

Typeset by The Harrington Consultancy Ltd
Printed in Great Britain by Bell and Bain Ltd., Glasgow.

Contents

DEDICATION
To Sam

Acknowledgements

I confess to having been somewhat daunted, when asked to write *Art for All*. Like all non-specialist teachers of art, I fell into the trap of imagining that the body of art knowledge and technical skill had eluded me. I soon realised that was the very point of this book: to access principles of art education to other non-specialist teachers of art working with pupils with wide-ranging needs. Whilst I am only too aware of my short-comings in terms of technical art expertise, this book, at very least, is grounded in tried and trusted practice. I'd like to thank all my colleagues and pupils over the years, who have taught me (almost!) everything I know, and at whose expense this book has been researched!

I am grateful to all those eminent authorities on art and special education who have faith and confidence in my skills and abilities as a teacher of art. I am indebted to my colleagues in Norfolk's Arts in Education Service for their constant support and all the stimulating debates which keep my practice constantly developing. In particular, I'd like to thank David Sheppard and Keith Winser for their help and advice on the drafts for this book. I am especially pleased that Keith has made a contribution to *Art for All*, on using Information Technology with pupils with learning difficulties. I'd also like to thank friends and teaching colleagues who have also offered comments on the drafts. I am indebted, as well, to Jillian Tearoe, for all her assistance with the diagrams.

I'd like to thank two artists, Beatrice Hoffman and Jai Chaudhuri, for their permission to reproduce their work in *Art for All*. Additionally, I'd like to thank them for the insights and vision that I have gained from working with them in a professional capacity, and for the inspiration they have given to staff and pupils of all abilities. I'd also like to acknowledge the co-operation of the copyright departments of the Tate Gallery and National Gallery, in procuring reproductions of some of their works. Thanks also to Stan Smith for his permission to draw from some of his work.

A special thank you is owed to the following children, whose work illustrates *Art for All*: Hayley Allen, Lynsey Attoe, Fleur Batson, Justine Botton, Mark Bristow, Katie Brown, Claire Burke, Sarah Corper, Matthew Cox, Jo-Ann Crutch, Pamela Dent, Lucie Dowson, Carl Glover, Samantha Grigg, Steven Grimmer, Aaron Haddon, John Hall, Christopher Jones, Searn Kearns, Aaron Mulholland, Helen Palmer, Sarah Parsons, Govind Patel, Alison Raven, Neil Rowson, Sally Shannon, Jesse Sheppard, Sam Sheppard, Hayley Sheey, Melanie Taylor, Tara Thraxton and David Wright.

Finally, I am grateful once again for all the support from my family whilst I have been working on the manuscript for this book. In particular, I'd like to thank my eldest son Sam, for keeping me constantly on my mettle, and reminding me of the sheer value and enjoyment art can bring to children. His enthusiasm and flair fuel my commitment to enabling the creative potential of children of all abilities to flourish. The pictures illustrating *Art for All* stand as testimony to my conviction. I hope this book may help others to feel similarly motivated.

Introduction

Art for All is a practical approach to art *teaching* that harnesses mainstream theory and practice to place art firmly in the curriculum for pupils with special educational needs. It aims to present a developmental framework for art with pupils with wide-ranging learning difficulties in the context of the National Curriculum, with strategies for structuring and supporting appropriate art activity. It is presented in two volumes: *The Framework* and *The Practice*. Whilst they stand as independent texts, they are intended to be used in conjunction. Together, they offer guidance on developing an area of the curriculum which has received less attention than others within special education in recent years.

Many teachers experience an inner conflict over their role as a mediator in art activity with pupils with learning difficulties: concerned not to intrude into what may be a personal experience and possibly a cathartic form of expression for the child, yet committed as educationalists that they should be enabling pupils to progress. The DES (1991) endorses the relevance of the National Curriculum to pupils of *all* abilities:

> It is our firm belief that all pupils should be able to benefit from their art education at school. If this belief is to be realised and the level of achievement of all pupils improved, particular attention needs to be given to certain groups of pupils who may find it difficult to realise their full potential. (para. 11.1, p 59)

But how? The National Curriculum (DFE, 1995) indicates the kind of opportunities pupils should be offered, in order to progress in different aspects of investigating and making, and knowing and understanding about art. *Art for All – The Framework* offers a structure in the light of National Curriculum requirements, on which to hang practice in relation to pupils whose development may be in very small steps, and by which their achievements may be recognised. Chapter 1 begins to set the context for developing art practice in relation to pupils with learning difficulties, and to illuminate the thinking behind the requirements of the National Curriculum. It considers the value of art in the curriculum, and aims of art education in relation to pupils with learning difficulties, with reference also to the teacher's role in effecting quality in learning and quality in teaching.

Chapter 2 looks more closely at development in art-making, and how children may progress in communicating ideas, feelings and meanings through visual and tactile means. It breaks down into manageable steps aspects of art-making identified in the National Curriculum – recording responses, gathering resources and materials, exploring and using art media, and reviewing and modifying work.

The key to pupils' development is their growing understanding and use of the elements of art. The National Curriculum recognises how these art elements are often closely associated: pattern and texture; colour; line and tone; shape, form and space. Chapters 3, 4, 5 and 6 look at the elements of art in associated groupings in more depth, and consider how pupils' progress may be recognised and their needs accommodated. These chapters, effectively, also offer a basic grounding in art theory, for the benefit of empowering non-specialist teachers to feel more confident in their practice. Pupils need to be enabled to progress in *using* the elements of art to make images and artefacts in a range of different media, in two and three dimensions. In this way, they may be equipped with a visual language with which to communicate their intentions.

Society is becoming increasingly reliant on direct visual communication. The National Curriculum stipulates that pupils should be taught to 'read images' – to become 'visually literate', to be empowered to make sense of their world. Pupils' understanding and enjoyment of art, craft and design should be developed as far as possible, through experiences that bring together their knowledge and understanding of the work of artists from a variety of cultures and traditions, in a way that inspires and informs their own art-making. Chapter 7 suggests strategies to enable pupils of all abilities to progress in understanding the work of other artists and in applying knowledge to their own work, and to respond to and evaluate art.

The Appendix comprises two recording sheets, one for noting pupils' overall progress in art, and the second, specifically, for noting progress in understanding and using the elements of art, expounded in depth during this volume. Judging pupils' achievements may be usefully cross referenced to benchmarks of development identified in the relevant chapters of this book: respectively, the art elements (chapters 3, 4, 5, and 6); art-making (chapter 2) and understanding and appreciating art (chapter 7).

Art for All is written by a convert to art teaching for non-art specialists, with the intention of demystifying principles of art education in practice with pupils with wide-ranging learning needs. The National Curriculum (DFE, 1995) intends 'art' to be interpreted as 'art, craft and design'. *Art for All* is *not* intended as a comprehensive manual. Those basic art practices are prioritised that are indicated in the National Curriculum: drawing, painting, print-making, collage and sculpture/3D. These are within the grasp of the non-specialist teacher of art without formal art training or grounding in particular techniques. However, teachers need to be aware of other forms of art-making not considered in depth in this book, and tap into in-service training courses and the services of artists with particular skills; for example, in ceramics, photography, architecture, graphic design, etc.

Art for All is aimed particularly at those practitioners working with pupils with learning difficulties – from profound and multiple learning difficulties (PMLD) to severe learning difficulties (SLD) and moderate learning difficulties (MLD). It is grounded in classroom practice, based on ten years' experience 'at the chalk face' and in delivering in-service training to meet the needs of teachers working in this challenging field. Effectively, however, it considers development in art equivalent to progress through Key Stages 1 and 2 in the National Curriculum. Hopefully, therefore, this handbook will be of interest also to those working in mainstream nursery and primary phases, as well as special education – indeed, all those committed to 'art for all'.

CHAPTER 1

Art in the Curriculum

The 'State of the Art'

Many teachers in special education have become acutely conscious in recent years of entitlement and empowerment issues for their pupils. Traditionally in the education of pupils with special needs, art has been regarded as 'good for them'. Art activity has been considered an opportunity for pupils to make a statement, significantly in a non-verbal form, when many of them struggle literally to 'have a voice'. There has been a strong pervasive feeling that art is to do with individual expression, and as such is in direct conflict with notions of teacher intervention. The emergence of art therapy as a discipline in recent years has highlighted the potentially cathartic emotional release through art activity. There is a 'grey area' between art teachers and art therapists in their work within special educational contexts:

- Both recognise the therapeutic value of the art process itself, for releasing tension or supporting the containment of feelings.
- Both encourage children's discovery of their creative 'live' side.
- By accepting a child's piece of work as communication or expression, both the art teacher as well as the art therapist may be providing a valuable opportunity for pupils' self-discovery, and to increase their self-esteem.
- Both may be helping children to make order out of chaos by taming messy materials, and making them work as a source of stimulation; this may be of particular significance to certain children whose lives lack structure and consistent support (based on Prokofiev, 1994).

The overlap between art therapy and art education is significant and should be recognised and acknowledged in practice. However, this has tended to make teachers all the more reluctant to intervene in the art-making process, as many teachers have been uncertain about their role or function. Inadvertently, highly laudable aspirations may have actually served to undermine the development of art *teaching* with pupils with learning difficulties.

Happily, however, much art activity has still been carried out in schools, even if 'ad hoc' in terms of planning or content of the activity. The tendency has been to link art with topic work in an illustrative kind of way, rather than to consider pupils' development in art itself. At very least, art has been considered an antidote to intensive teaching programmes focusing on objective skills that have characterised curriculum development in other areas in special education during the 1980s. Art did not fit comfortably into tick boxes, and was left behind at a time when other areas of the curriculum were being tightly defined.

Into the 1990s, the balance is being redressed. The National Curriculum, with its aspirations for 'breadth and balance', has given status and recognition to art as a foundation subject in its own right - 'art for art's sake'. However, the 1980s have left their legacy. For a long time, art has suffered from being low priority on teacher training courses. This has had implications for art teaching, particularly with the closure of initial courses for working with pupils with learning difficulties towards the end of the 1980s. The upshot is that teachers working in this field are often non-art specialists, and insufficiently prepared for meeting their pupils' needs. Equally, many teachers feel ill-equipped for meeting the demands of accountability for their pupils' progress in the light of the National Curriculum.

Whilst 'enabling' in the sense that pupils of all abilities may be embraced by the document, the National Curriculum Art Order (DFE, 1995) provides little assistance in identifying progress *within* different aspects of art. Neither does it identify progress in small enough steps for the achievements to be recognised of those pupils whose progress may be patchy and/or relatively slow. Issues relating to teaching methodology have been removed. Whilst this is meant to be liberating for the teacher, it leaves those working with pupils with learning difficulties still struggling to provide a fine balance between repetition and variety of activity to meet the needs of those pupils progressing in terms of *breadth* of experience, who may remain at a particular stage for a long time.

The National Curriculum advocates that teachers should set aims and objectives in relation to strands comprising Programmes of Study (POS). End of Key Stage Descriptions (EKSDs) are *not* intended to be used as benchmarks for setting curriculum aims and objectives. Rather, they are meant to be used essentially as a reporting tool against which teachers may make 'best fit' judgements concerning a pupil's attainment. For example, at Key Stages 1 and 2, attainment is supposed to correlate to some notional levels 2 and 4 respectively. This effectively links them with age-related 'norms', which may risk disadvantaging pupils with learning difficulties since their achievements may be regarded negatively. This is a shame, given the intention to make POS more flexible, so that pupils may work in the Key Stage most suited to their ability.

Nevertheless, in principle at least, the National Curriculum is committed to the notion of one 'art for all'. Key Stage POS have been written such that there are aspects that can be taught to all pupils in ways appropriate to their abilities, with the proviso that material presented is age-appropriate in its content and context. It is the job of the teacher to translate National Curriculum requirements into classroom practice. This begs the question as to *what* actually constitutes progress? Is it being able to do things that are increasingly more complex? Or is it doing the *same* thing but better? Or the same thing, but with increasing awareness and understanding of the process involved? And how can teachers be enabled to plan sufficiently challenging, developmentally appropriate activities, so that the artistic process can flourish?

Art and Child Development

In a frequently quoted phrase, Gombrich (1972) once said 'there is no such thing as art – there are only artists'. This can be taken as an exhortation to value the *process* of art-making. For children, art can be a way of learning (see figure 1.1):

- communication of something that is significant, related to the child's environment and experience – a fusion between expression and the emotions of the young artist;
- an integrating experience – a reflection of children's organisational ability and how they make sense of their world, which may become consolidated through the art activity;
- a two-way learning process, as children paint (or draw) what they experience (objects and/or events) and experience what they paint.

Figure 1.1: *'A house, a roof, a door, window and a spaceship, a tiger and a lion, it is raining' (felt-pen drawing by an infant pupil with severe learning difficulties). An example of how the artist interacts with and is influenced by the media during the art-making process.*

Patterns of development in children's art are well documented (see *Art for All – The Practice*, chapter 1). Rate of progress through developmental stages will be affected by environmental factors and materials available, children's experiences and intellectual development, *not* their chronological age; particular disabling conditions and emotional stability may also be contributory factors. Some pupils with learning difficulties may not be out of line with their mainstream peers with regard to their artistic development. The work of Stephen Wiltshire (the boy with autism who draws buildings) is a notable example of the exceptional artistic *ability* certain pupils with learning difficulties may have. Many children with learning difficulties, however, may take a very long time to pass through a stage of development in art. They will need plenty of time and scope to explore any one stage. Teachers therefore, need to think in terms of *broadening experiences* at any one stage.

Children will also be affected by the *art medium*, as this can promote different kinds of response. For example, finger paints, even in the hands of developmentally mature artists, will encourage a smearing, more emotional abstract response, which may belie an ability also for precise detailed work in a different medium such as a sketching pencil. Materials selected for an activity should not inhibit or obstruct self-expression, as this can affect progress and growth in art (compare figures 1.2 and 1.3 p.9). There needs to be plenty of opportunity for drawing and painting, as these media best facilitate children's ability to think, reason and organise. 'Novelty' activities, including many so-called 'craft' activities (such as making angels out of toilet rolls), tend to offer limited opportunities for individual creative expression, as they often place too much emphasis on an end-product – indeed, a creative input by a child may even risk being regarded as a 'mistake'. Such work can often display little variation or risk minimal differentiation according to pupils' developmental level and their creative potential.

It is a moot point, however, to what extent certain pupils with learning difficulties would acquire a repertoire of using the art elements (colour, pattern, texture, line, etc) spontaneously, without being presented with possibilities by an adult. Focusing solely on particular skills, such as copying stereotyped images or shapes, will *not* lead to increased *artistic* competence in the child. They may well be valid as a perceptual exercise, for improving hand-eye co-ordination. Arguably, however, *creative* development may become stunted, because the child may become dependent on adult concepts which may be alien to the child's own schema. Awareness and formation of shapes will emerge from developing self-expression. Children need to learn how a visual language can become ordered to convey meaning:

> Pupils need to understand the visual conventions associated with each art form and the ways in which they can be used in order to become fluent in their use of the visual language... The ability to see clearly and to draw, paint, model and handle the associated technical problems is essential in a world that relies increasingly on direct visual communication. (DES, 1991, p 9)

The Value of Art in the Curriculum

The DES (1991) places art in the context of the whole curriculum, and considers links between art and other subjects and implications for cross-curricular work. This is also recognised by OFSTED (1994), particularly in the promotion of pupils' spiritual, moral, social and cultural development, which it regards as a 'whole school' issue. For example, pupils' capacity for reflection and curiosity, and a sense of awe and wonder may be actively promoted when pupils consider their own art-making and works of other artists. OFSTED (1994) affirms the National Curriculum attainment targets as the basis for making judgements of standards in art, in respect of investigating and making (Attainment Target 1) and knowledge and understanding (Attainment Target 2). The following aims for art education for *all* pupils underpin the Programmes of Study proposed in the Art Order (DFE, 1995). Art education should:

- enable pupils to become visually literate: to use and understand art as a form of visual and tactile communication and to have confidence and competence in reading and evaluating visual images and artefacts;
- develop particular creative and technical skills so that ideas can be realised and artefacts produced;
- develop pupils' aesthetic sensibilities and enable them to make informed judgements about art;
- develop pupils' design capability;
- develop pupils' capacity for imaginative and original thought and experimentation;
- develop pupils' capacity to learn about and observe the world in which they live;
- develop pupils' ability to articulate and communicate ideas, opinions and feelings about their own work and that of others;
- develop pupils' ability to value the contribution made by artists, craftworkers and designers and to respond thoughtfully, critically and imaginatively to ideas, images and objects of many kinds and from many cultures. (DES, 1991, para. 4.1, p 17)

Some key concepts

Visual literacy

This is the understanding of how the elements of art may be used to communicate ideas, feelings and meanings; it is particularly significant and potentially empowering for pupils with learning difficulties in preparing them to deal with insight with the likely bombardment of visual imagery through their lives in a world that relies increasingly on direct visual communication. Pupils need to learn to 'read' an artist's intentions (implicit and explicit), and how to convey their own messages in different art media.

Imagination

This is a capacity to explore and experiment with memory, and to combine ideas rationally or irrationally as a form of creative, divergent thinking. In the case of certain pupils with learning difficulties, the time-gap may need to be very short indeed between recalling a past experience and experimenting with memory in a creative way. 'Working from the imagination', therefore, is not necessarily about projecting themselves into fantasy or an activity which they have not personally experienced (e.g. 'a walk on the moon'). Imaginative work of quality is more likely to arise from recall of direct experiences. The importance of ensuring that pupils have a reservoir of experiences from which to select, and of building up 'aides memoires' in the form of secondary reference resource material, will be crucial.

Aesthetic knowing

This is really to do with learning through the senses, verbally and non-verbally, not just concern with notions of taste and beauty as implied in NCC documentation (DES, 1991). The implications of this for pupils with learning difficulties are to endorse a multi-sensory approach for direct experiences which may inform pupils' art-making; equally, that the 'hands-on' nature of the art-making process itself may prompt aesthetic knowing.

Art and craft, design and technology

These areas have become closely linked in recent years in the eyes of the architects of curriculum processes. The drive has stemmed from emergent vocational aspirations, closely allied to the notion of a creative attitude to problem-solving as a desirable entity. Artists, craftspeople and designers need to take account of functional and economic considerations (time, cost, materials, etc) and appeal of a product. Implicit is the development of practical understanding and application of possible solutions to challenges, and the notion of visualising potential outcomes – whether ultimately successful or unsuccessful – and learning from experience. In relation to pupils with learning difficulties, it can be a particularly pertinent, empowering notion to have a grasp of a range of options and the viability of particular materials for a particular purpose, with an understanding of the implications of their use. Design and technology can be considered as *aspects* of art education – but not substitutes for it.

Implications for Teaching Art

The teacher of art needs to be an *enabler* and provider of knowledge and resources. In mainstream secondary education, most art teachers have degree status, in order to be able to offer pupils a level of technical expertise. However, a teacher without specialist training in art may still achieve a great deal with developmentally young pupils, by harnessing methods and approaches in good art teaching. It is more important to establish a conducive atmosphere, not where there may be a 'right response', but where pupils may feel that they are collaborating in a venture, motivated and inspired by their teacher's commitment and enthusiasm. Teachers have an obligation to ensure quality learning by pupils and that good standards are achieved in art, taking account of pupils' relative ability to record what they have seen, imagined or recalled. Pupils' responses should be regarded as valid statements in their own right, not as an inferior form of adult art. OFSTED (1994) indicates criteria by which *quality* teaching in art may be ascertained, that teachers should:

- *Ensure that pupils undertake a balanced programme of art, craft and design activities which clearly builds on previous work and takes account of previous achievement.* This demands that teachers are aware of patterns of growth in art, and are able to plan and implement developmentally appropriate activities, with a clear sense of direction regarding their pupils' needs. Teachers need to be aware of how pupils may progress in the different forms of art-making, in two- *and* three-dimensional work. Three-dimensional work is particularly important for learning about scale and proportion, and for managing tools and materials. Teachers need to be able to analyse procedures involved in art-making into sufficiently small steps to cater for the needs of pupils of all abilities, and to differentiate activities to meet individual needs.

- *Ensure that pupils are able to work independently, in groups and as a whole class.* Some pupils with learning difficulties often tend to lack creative drive. Teachers will need to ensure first-hand experiences of the natural and made environment, backed up with reference material (objects, photographs, sketches 'in the field', etc), to inspire and inform pupils at their art-making. Art activities will need to be carefully structured and differentiated, to enable pupils to make creative choices and decisions, to select resources and share equipment, and to organise themselves as autonomously as possible. Pupils' confidence and pleasure in art-making will develop through learning to control and use a *limited* range of tools and materials, rather than superficially experimenting with a bewildering array. The introduction of new equipment needs to be sensitively paced, with the range available gradually broadened, to enable pupils to work in open-ended tasks involving a suitable level of 'risk-taking'. Staff will need to be allocated to support individuals and groups of pupils, but sufficiently briefed to prevent them from dominating the activities. Pupils of all abilities should experience working at individual and collaborative pieces.

- *Give pupils explanations and demonstrations of techniques and processes appropriate to each stage of the learning process.* All pupils with learning difficulties, to greater or lesser degree, will experience problems in assimilating a 'verbal flow'. Instruction needs to be succinctly presented and clearly illustrated with visual aids. Abstract concepts should be used selectively and supported with reference to 'concrete' objects and images. Teachers need to be aware of steps involved in an art-making activities, in order to present pupils with tasks that are developmentally appropriate. Complex procedures that require pupils to follow precise sequences may prove too challenging and beyond the grasp of certain individuals. Teachers need to consider how an activity may be 'revisited', with challenges gradually broadened and/or increased to extend and improve pupils' perception and practical skill. This should take account of pupils' progress through developmental stages in art, and their increasing confidence and ability to handle tools and materials, and to follow procedures for working in a range of media.

- *Provide a sequence of structured activities including a range of opportunities for pupils to create their own art work as well as to carry out written, oral and research tasks.* Teachers need to ensure a balance between pupils' investigating and making art, and developing their knowledge and understanding of art. It is expected that proportionately, this will be reflected in a ratio of two to one, with opportunity for pupils to reflect on aspects of their own work and that of others. Sufficient *time* has to be afforded for pupils with learning difficulties, to make connections and to assimilate ideas. Pupils of all abilities should produce work that is original and personal, to use their memory and imagination. This may be 'fed' through direct experiences in ways indicated above, with staff sensitively supporting and guiding pupils' art-making. Teaching styles may have to be adapted: procedures repeated and re-presented using a multi-sensory approach, to accommodate individual needs such as short-term memory and visual or physical impairment.

- *Give direct instruction about the nature and history of art.* The work of other artists offers considerable enrichment potential, for the education of pupils of all abilities. Teachers need to access the work of other artists to their pupils, in order to inform them of their artistic heritage, and to inspire their art-making (see chapter 7). This may place considerable demands on teachers of pupils with learning difficulties, to present works of art from a variety of artistic traditions in a way that is relevant to their pupils' experience, needs and abilities. Pupils should experience a balance of art from a variety of cultures and contexts – western and world art. The work of other artists ought to be integrated with practical activities, where pupils are encouraged to make connections both in and to their own work, and to explore and apply approaches and ideas in their own art-making.

- *Provide opportunities for art, craft and design to be seen in a context which has spiritual, moral, social and cultural relevance to pupils' own lives.* Teachers have a responsibility for ensuring that their pupils perceive art as having status and importance as a means for personal and cultural expression. Teachers' attitudes to art will be revealed explicitly and implicitly: through the way it is taught, and how it is presented in the school environment. Pupils' work should be displayed thoughtfully, with pride and esteem set on the achievements of pupils of all abilities. Teachers are obliged to plan art into the timetable, with opportunities for pupils to develop their artistic ability and understanding in their own right. Teachers need to consider the extent to which they are trained, informed and confident in delivering and differentiating all aspects of art to pupils with wide-ranging learning difficulties. Issues of equality need to be addressed: regard to art from a range of cultures and traditions, abstract and naturalistic, two- and three-dimensional, with work by both male and female artists, and accessed in a way that is meaningful to the pupils. This may be reinforced through effective use of local artists, galleries and museums. Pupils' practical work and verbal responses should reveal sensitive and informed reactions both to their own work and that of others.

- *Provide pupils with a learning environment which stimulates and supports visual investigation and provides for the safe development of practical skills.* Pupils' imagination and inventiveness at all levels of ability may be promoted, enriched and challenged through displays of pupils' work and that of other artists. Pupils will also require visual and tactile resources and multi-sensory displays, to inspire and inform the art-making process; for example, natural and made objects and artefacts, walk-in environments and 'corners', and pictorial reference material. The classroom environment needs to be structured and orderly, to enable pupils of all abilities to negotiate their working space confidently and as independently as possible, with effective use made of designated areas. An ethos should be encouraged whereby everyone is mindful of the safety of others, and takes responsibility for keeping the environment clean and tidy, with items replaced after use. Staff and pupils need to have access to a range of art equipment, and to be aware of using tools and materials judiciously and economically, and with respect. Tools and materials should be sufficiently varied and challenging, and of a suitable quality, to foster pupils' art-making and to develop their skills (in 2D, 3D and their use of IT). There should also be access to a range of resources for teaching historical and critical aspects of art: collections of prints and reproductions, books and slides of western and world art.

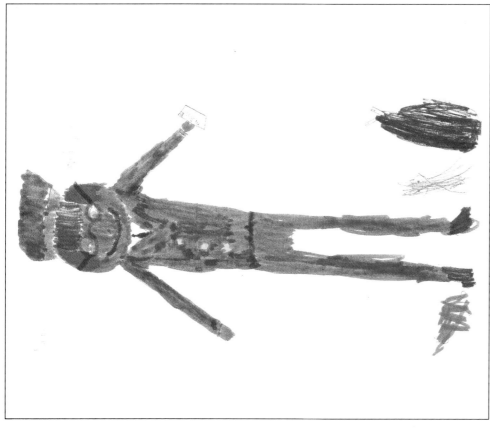

Figure 1.3: *'Postman Pat' (felt-pen drawing by six year old pupil in mainstream). These two images were created by the same pupil within 24 hours of each other. They clearly illustrate the effect of the medium on a pupil's artistic expression – the choice of colours in figure 1.2 had been prescribed by the teacher and offered limited scope for creating new combinations, paint brushes were too thick to allow for detailed work, with no opportunity for the pupil to return to and modify his work using other materials. The pupil found the felt pens in figure 1.3 much easier to control, and that they lent themselves to details.*

Figure 1.2: *A self-portrait (painting by six year old pupil in mainstream).*

Figure 2.2: *'The Snail' (1953), by Henri Matisse (Tate Gallery, London) (collage in cut and torn paper). Matisse had become physically disabled by the time he executed this work. It was achieved from his wheelchair, with large pieces of glued, brightly coloured paper affixed onto the wall using long sticks. © Succession H. Matisse/DACS1996*

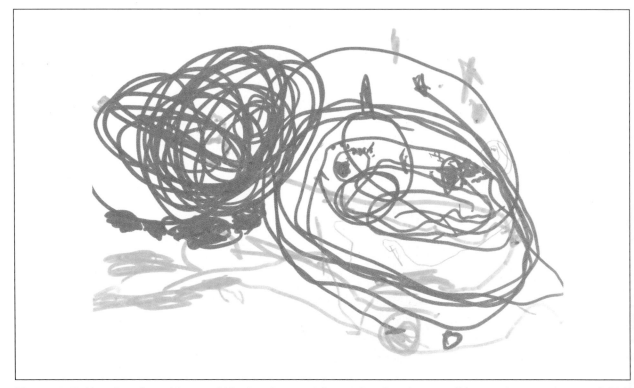

Figure 2.3: *'A red engine with a truck' (red and green felt pen drawing, by a pupil in a mainstream nursery). This boy had been playing with models of trains from the popular children's books about Thomas the Tank Engine. The marks he made reminded him of James the red engine; he modified his work in process to include the trucks.*

Figure 6.6: *The Coast'* (group collage by junior pupils with severe learning difficulties). In assembling this class frieze, the teacher has observed certain rules of composition to give a sense of depth: the figures project beyond the format, to draw the viewer into the picture; the clothing is in 'hot' colours which apparently 'advance' compared to the background; the figures project into the line of the horizon, which focuses the viewer's gaze on the images, rather than be distracted it along an unbroken horizon and out of frame; the foreground (sand dunes) has been given more texture and contoured (newspaper stuffed behind); the figures have been placed centrally to give a strong sense of symmetry, and to focus the viewer's attention primarily on them.

Figure 3.3: 'A Chinese junk' (group frieze by junior pupils with severe learning difficulties). A range of experiences in creating textures and patterns have been combined: irregular salt-trailing patterns (the sea), breaking the surface of cromar paint with cardboard combs (the sky), sticking clusters of painted art straws in regular rows (the wooden boat), pleating paper (the sails), cutting out and arranging paper oblongs in regular rows (the buildings).

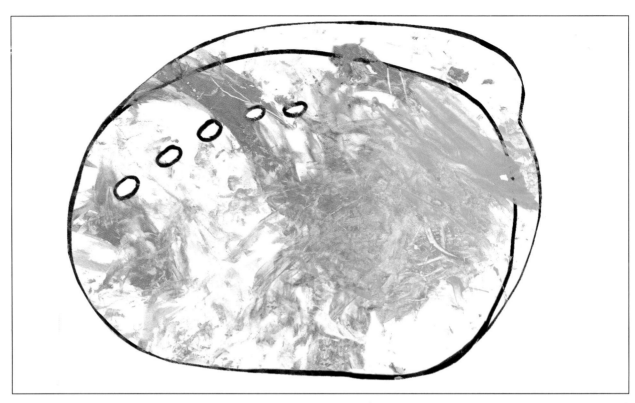

Figure 3.1: *Finger-painting based on the texture of a mother-of-pearl shell (iridescent finger-paints, by a pupil with profound and moderate learning difficulties). The pupil had explored a large mother-of-pearl shell (looking at it, feeling it, holding it, etc) immediately beforehand. The paper was prepared in the same shape as the shell (complete with air holes) before the pupil made her marks, and paints pre-selected which might resonate with the previous experience for her, to be (literally) re-presented in art-making.*

Figure 3.2: *'Cowrie shell' (painting by junior pupil with moderate learning difficulties). This pupil selected and worked directly from the shell; she requested a guideline to keep her pattern even.*

CHAPTER 2

The Art-Making Process

Development in
Art-Making

The art of children with learning difficulties indicates a similar pattern of development to that of their mainstream peers; however, the actual *ages* at which changes occur may vary considerably. Pupils' development in art, however, is not an inevitable process: it requires teachers to provide opportunities in which the creative process may flourish. Teachers need to have a clear grasp of developmental stages in art, and teaching strategies to meet individual pupils' needs to enable them to progress, with consideration for those pupils who may 'plateau' for a considerable time. However.....

> Children must proceed at their own pace. Knowing the stages gives us the opportunity to match activities to what the children are capable of producing, and avoids forcing upon them those images for which they are not yet ready. The fixed blue line at the top of a painting and the green one at the bottom are sky and grass until children are ready for it to be different. Faces are painted blue, green or purple, until flesh colours seem important enough. Focusing their attention on the sky, or on flesh tones, but not demanding that sky meets ground, or that flesh is pink, encourages them to look and question what they see. The search must still be theirs, not ours. (Barnes, 1987, p 51-52)

The principles that Barnes advocates are as relevant to pupils with learning difficulties as to their mainstream peers. For many pupils with learning difficulties, however, it is a moot point to what extent they may or may not attain developmental milestones *spontaneously*. Some may not have the same natural drive and curiosity as their mainstream peers, nor make the kind of connections so readily that Barnes describes.

To a greater or lesser degree, all pupils with learning difficulties struggle with recall, perception and generalising and applying learning. They will need plenty of opportunities for first-hand direct experiences and for 'hands on' exploration of objects, artefacts and other stimuli, and experimentation with tools and materials. Pupils with learning difficulties will be dependent on such opportunities to reinforce their knowledge and understanding of their world, which may then become integrated and expressed through their art-making (see figure 2.1).

Figure 2.1: *'Dalek' (drawing in black felt pen, by senior pupil with severe learning difficulties). This drawing indicates how knowledge of an aspect of the artist's experience can inform art-making – compare the accuracy of the dalek (an obsessional interest) to other figurative images.*

Acquiring a Visual Language – the Elements of Art

The art elements are used in combination in different forms of art making. For example, Matisse's collage in cut and torn paper pieces entitled 'The Snail' (see figure 2.2 p.10), makes particular use of *shape* (regular geometric squares and oblongs), *space* (strategic placement of large pieces over a large background), *colour* (choice of bright primary and secondary hues) and *pattern* (spiral arrangement). Pupils' attention may also be deliberately focused at various times, in art forms which emphasise a particular element: for example, colour in painting, line in drawing, form in sculpture, etc. By offering a variety of tools and techniques with which to work in different kinds of art activities, pupils will experience opportunities to develop their ability to use the range of different art elements. If pupils only ever experienced two-dimensional drawing in pencil, their potential development would be impoverished.

However, in planning art experiences, teachers of pupils with learning difficulties should take account of their individual needs in respect of their ability to use the different art elements. Their relative progress in using the different art elements may well be lop-sided. The teacher will need to work to pupils' strengths in order to maximise their potential powers of expression through art. For example, the development of blind children's ability to understand how colour is applied and experienced is likely not to be as advanced as their ability to use texture and three-dimensional form. In the case of blind children, teachers may prioritise collage and sculpture, as these forms of art-making will best enable the pupils to integrate their knowledge of the physical world through the sense of touch, and to express a response to it.

Physically impaired children may struggle with the fine motor co-ordination required to control tools and materials to produce (for example) subtleties of line and tone and intricacies of pattern, even if conceptually they have a grasp of how these may be achieved in different art forms. Teachers will need to make it possible for physically impaired children to make creative decisions based on their level of understanding of how the art elements may be used. For example, using computer software may enable such pupils to produce a range of lines, thus liberating them to produce drawings that reflect their level of creative decision making (see *Art for All – The Practice*, chapter 5). Using the art elements in abstract forms of expression may free pupils to make interpretations prompted by sophisticated conceptual thinking, but which emphasise the use of other elements (e.g. colour and shape) as opposed to line and tone in more naturalistic interpretations. Matisse's paper cuts (see figure 2.2 p.10) were achieved late in his lifetime, when he had become physically impaired.

Pupils need to acquire a visual language that will be as rich and varied as possible, through working in a range of media, but balanced with sufficient opportunities to develop their abilities confidently in activities that are familiar. Teachers of pupils with learning difficulties need to be aware of their pupils' relative progress in the different art elements, and address areas of weakness as well as working to pupils' strengths in ways indicated above. Art-making will *integrate* children's ability to use the art elements; this will be reflected in the way these are combined and ordered to communicate ideas, feelings and meanings. It is the teacher's responsibility to structure appropriate art experiences that will enable pupils to progress in their understanding and *use* of their visual language.

Investigating and Making Art – Using the Visual Language

A professional artist may spend weeks, months, years maybe, over one piece of work. Making art takes *effort* – a creative form of expression that conveys the artist's intention as accurately as possible. Pupils need to acquire the sense of satisfaction that comes from such creative endeavour. The teacher is responsible for developing this attitude towards art-making in pupils by bestowing respect and status on their work, and encouraging pupils to relish in the challenges posed by an art activity. There needs to be a spirit of adventure, with a creative attitude to 'mistakes' and 'problems'. These challenges need to be 'solvable' and appropriate for the child's stage of development – for example, trying to impose perspective drawing on pupils whose representational images were just emerging would be alien to their schema, and damaging to their confidence and self-esteem.

Potentially, as children develop in their concentration and in the way they perceive and order their world, as well as in their technical ability to use tools and materials, so this may become reflected in their art-making: children may become capable of spending longer over a piece of work, with more concern for detail and accuracy. It is the teacher's responsibility to ensure that circumstances are conducive for pupils to progress. Ultimately, pupils need to be enabled to set themselves appropriate challenges in their art-making, at whatever stage they may reach or strive for, and equipped with strategies for coping with these self-imposed challenges.

Recording responses

Pupils of all abilities need to learn how they may record experiences in art, based on first-hand observation and analysis of features in the environment. It stands to reason that in order to record their responses pupils have to experience something to which to respond. Prerequisites, therefore, for pupils' art-making will be direct experiences in different environments, and 'hands on' exploration of objects, artefacts and materials. The time-gap between an experience and follow-up art work will be particularly significant for pupils with learning difficulties, especially with regard to problems with recall and memory span. The materials offered to pupils with which to record their responses will also have a bearing, and may inherently encourage a response that harnesses particular art elements (e.g. colour in paint, line in charcoal, shape in cut paper, pattern and/or texture in fabrics, etc). Techniques should be offered with challenges appropriate to pupils' growing proficiency with procedures and control of tools and materials, and an expanding range of options on processes for art-making.

1 *Multi-sensory exploration of tools and materials* may prompt a response in abstract expression; this is particularly significant for pupils at early stages in their art-making. For example, trailing fingers through finger paint to produce an abstract design, or poking with an oblong brick into clay to create abstract patterns.

2 Pupils may progress to engaging in *art-making activity immediately following a direct experience* and/or opportunity to handle an object or artefact as a stimulus, where the art-making may indicate the influence and impact of the previous experience. Pupils will need experiences and events to prompt them to make a conceptual leap: that these may be communicated and literally 're-presented' through art. This cannot (and should not) be forced. By following up an experience immediately with an art activity, it may be that in the course of mark-making, something resonates and triggers the pupil's memory whilst it is still fresh. This may help pupils make the connection that marks may be used representationally or to evoke an aspect of an experience (e.g. the colour of certain objects), even if at first images are not recognisable to the viewer (see figure 2.3 p.10).

3 Pupils may *recall a previous experience, and use this as a basis for engaging in art-making*. Pupils' early representational work tends to be important images reproduced from memory, indicating those features of most significance to the child. This may be 'fed' by providing memorable experiences as a fund from which the pupils may (literally!) draw, followed up as soon as possible with an art activity. For example, following a trip to a fire station, a pupil engaged in three-dimensional construction using 'found' sources may spontaneously state that he or she is making a fire engine. The previous experience may also be an art activity; for example, a pupil may ask to make

a 'squash' print, by folding in half a paint-spattered piece of paper, to produce a symmetrical pattern.

4 Pupils may progress to *working from direct, first-hand observation,* referring to a stimulus to inform their art-making. Pupils may be helped to notice features in the natural and made environments: their attention drawn to details of pattern, colour, decoration, etc. These may inspire naturalistic or abstract work. Pupils may be encouraged to work 'in situ' from real objects, and to use sketch books when out 'in the field' on school trips, as a means to record and note responses immediately. For example, drawing a variegated leaf using coloured pencils; moulding a cup in new clay and painting a design when dry, in the geometric style of Clarice Cliff's 'Bizarre' range.

5 As their memory span expands, pupils may be challenged to *refer to secondary resource material to support their art-making.* They may need 'aides-mémoire' in the form of photographs, video or souvenirs to recollect an experience. They may develop their use of sketch books as their own 'aide-mémoire', from which to refer subsequently to inform and support their art-making back at school: to reproduce images from memory, with their sketch books as reference. Pupils may be encouraged to record their responses both in naturalistic and more abstract ways. For example, mixing tonal ranges from a limited palette referring to sketches and photographs of autumn leaves observed on a school trip, then painting bands of colour to make an abstract design based on a leaf motif, or naturalistic leaves with regard to accuracy of detail.

6 Pupils may use *secondary resource material as a stimulus* for their own interpretations. The work of other artists may inspire pupils with a range of possibilities for recording responses. For example, pupils may consider reproductions of Monet's paintings of his lily pond, then sketch the school pond and experiment with the Impressionist technique of making dots and dabs of paint, before painting their own interpretation of the pond in an Impressionist style. The elements of art may also be used for their own sake; for example, referring to photographs of zebras, as the basis for monochrome abstract designs using string on black paper.

Gathering resources

Pupils need to know how to collect and use resources to inform and/or inspire their art-making. They may progress from using pre-selected resources, to taking responsibility themselves for amassing reference materials that will stimulate and inform their art-making. Pupils need to understand that people, objects, places and events can be represented in two and three dimensions in a range of media. Much ground work may be necessary to establish pupils' symbolic concept, to enable them to relate on a variety of scales to photographs, pictures, miniature representations, life-size models and larger-than-life sculptures. This will enable pupils to recognise images, objects and artefacts as a possible source of ideas, inspiration and reference material for naturalistic and abstract work in two and three dimensions.

Works by other artists may be used as a *starting-point* with pupils, to illustrate possible interpretations on a theme (naturalistic and/or abstract), and to remind them that their own work does not have to look like a photographic likeness. Also, pupils may wish to work from them to explore a particular technique. However, this should lead to pupils harnessing approaches in their *own* work, to make their *own* interpretations (see chapter 7).

1 Pupils with learning difficulties may be challenged from relating to realistic representations (e.g. photographs, naturalistc drawings and life-like sculptures), to *identifying images and partial images* in increasingly more abstract work. For example, they may be asked to identify familiar objects in the work of other artists. This needs to be paralleled by the pupils' discovery of and familiarity with different forms of art-making, and the potential for expressing ideas, feelings and meanings in different media. For example, they may indicate that they wish to do a painting, or sign 'painting' on observing a work in their environment.

2 Pupils may be encouraged consciously to build on and follow up direct experiences and 'hands on' exploration of objects and artefacts, by *incorporating items directly in their art-making*. In this way, they may grasp that experiences may be 'captured' and 'represented' in art. For example, following a class trip to the seaside, pupils may make an abstract collage using sand and 'found sources' from beach-combing.

3 Pupils may progress to *using objects and artefacts directly as a source of ideas for their own work*. They may also develop the habit of collecting 'aides-mémoire' of experiences to bring to art-making, such as souvenirs, postcards and models, and photographs of a class outing. For example, pupils may handle shells of different kinds before selecting one as a stimulus for a drawing or painting, with particular attention to reproducing patterning (see figure 3.2 p.12).

4 Pupils need to learn that it will not always be feasible to have an object they may wish to represent (e.g. a spaceship), in front of them there and then from which to work! To avoid disillusionment setting in, or recoursing to pleading to an adult to do it for them, pupils may learn to *refer to a resource bank of secondary picture material*. Teachers may instigate a collection of postcards or photographs cut out from magazines mounted and laminated, sorted into categories (e.g. different kinds of animals, flowers, transport, etc). Teachers and pupils may also take their own photographs to build up the resource bank. Pupils should be involved in classification, and in contributing to the resource. It is important, ideally, that reference material is *not* pictures or interpretations by other people, however naturalistic – this will already have entailed a selection and editing process by the artist concerned.

5 Pupils may learn to work from first-hand observation, and *use a range of resources to support and inform their art-making*. For example, using their sketchbooks with confidence (noting significant details, colours, etc) to record observations and collect visual evidence and information, as a point of reference to support future work. Pupils may learn the value of backing this up with photographs of selected aspects of an experience.

6 Pupils may be made aware of the potential of *using resources in the community*, such as libraries, museums and galleries. Not only may these

have information and reference material, but also a range of interesting and unusual collections, objects and artefacts that will directly feed pupils' art-making. Pupils will need to learn how to use reference material selectively and creatively – to edit, refine and even change the original stimulus in their eventual interpretations in art. They may also wish to attend an adult education class, to develop a particular technique (e.g. pottery).

Exploring and using media

Pupils need to be aware of a range of options for their self-expression in and through art: to be proficient in a range of media for working in two and three-dimensional art forms on a variety of scales. Developing understanding and use of the elements of art will be given in depth consideration in chapters 3, 4, 5 and 6. Here, therefore, attention will be given to enabling pupils to learn how to structure and organise art activity for themselves as autonomously as possible, and to experiment with, explore and control a range of tools, techniques and materials.

Pupils with learning difficulties may need artistic techniques to be demonstrated step-by-step, before they are 'let loose' on an activity, and to be aware of possibilities for using the tools and materials. Whilst this may seem unduly directive, paradoxically, it may *enable* pupils to work creatively, if they have a clear grasp of procedures involved. Supporting staff need to be sensitive however: over-stating a procedure or, alternatively, presenting a bewildering range of options, may risk stunting pupils' exploration and experimentation. It stands to reason that the teacher needs to structure tasks, to take account of pupils' relative abilities to follow a sequence and retain procedures. For example, one pupil may find it easier if each pot of ready-mixed paint has its own separate brush, remembering to return it to the appropriate colour each time. Another pupil may be able to cope with a more complicated process: working up dry powder colour by combining it with water in a mixing palette, and remembering to wash the brush and squeeze out any excess on a rag before dipping in to a new colour.

1 Initially pupils need to learn to *recognise implements by name, to hold them correctly and to make controlled movements with them*, in order to use materials and tools in a range of techniques (2D and 3D). For example, cutting accurately and safely with scissors, managing brushes in a range of thicknesses and lengths, etc.

2 Pupils need to develop good work habits from the outset – to use implements safely, and to recognise the importance of keeping the working environment clean and orderly, and to *follow correct procedures for care of equipment*. Pupils should be instilled with the responsibility for organising themselves with tools and materials. Initially, they may need to follow a coded system. For example, they may locate a brush and water pot on request, by identifying pictorial symbols on storage cupboard doors.

3 Pupils may progress to following and *implementing basic art and craft techniques, with respect for the care and use of materials:* drawing, painting, collage, print-making and sculpture/3D work. For example, etching a design with a ball-point pen into a polystyrene tile printing block, and using

printing ink and roller to run off a series of prints, then cleaning equipment afterwards and returning items to respective store facilities.

4 Pupils need to *become 'fluent' in organising themselves independently for working in 'dry' techniques*. Activities involving 'dry' tools and materials will be easier in the main for pupils to prepare and to have control of their use in particular techniques (charcoal being a notable exception!). Pupils should work towards obtaining the materials they require from a freely available, clearly organised store. The range available needs to be structured, to enable pupils to make informed decisions and selections. For example, choosing a large or small piece of paper from a surface top will be easier than coping with the dazzling array of colours, shapes and sizes that may be available in the paper store. Gradually parameters may be widened, to increase the range from which the pupil is asked to select.

5 'Wet' procedures are more complicated – both in preparation and processes involved. Nevertheless, pupils should work towards *setting themselves up independently for 'wet' techniques,* preparing and protecting themselves and the work space appropriately, and controlling tools and materials in their use.

6 Being sufficiently versed in a range of materials, tools, techniques and procedures will enable pupils to *select an appropriate medium to achieve a particular intention, and to organise themselves independently* in their art-making. This may include familiarity with 'joining' techniques, such as glueing, nailing, tying, knotting, etc, with attention to matters of safety.

Reflecting on their work

Pupils need to develop the capacity to reflect on their work and make changes, taking on board or rejecting the comments of others, describing, criticising and expressing opinions. Potentially, this is a very empowering notion: giving children explicit control over their own art-making, and in planning future work. Teachers are often working under tremendous pressure, as many pupils with learning difficulties need considerable support and organisation. In one's urgency to give equal opportunity and regard for all members of the class, an art session inadvertently may be rushed through, with a quiet sense of relief if each child has 'done a picture' at the end. Misplaced good intentions may be valuing the product of an art activity at the expense of the process of art-making. This may not be the best way of proceeding!

If pupils are to be truly empowered, then the whole art-making process may need to be slowed down. Maybe a small group of pupils at a time should experience working in a more complicated art form (at least, in terms of the organisation involved), whilst others work in a different medium. This will make it possible for them to spend longer exploring a particular activity; at the following session, pupils may swap round. This will give everyone access to a breadth of opportunities for experiencing different forms of art-making. The point is, sufficient time *has* to be made for pupils to stand back from their work, refine techniques in process, share it with others, talk about it, discuss it and consider comments of others. This can be a fine line which teachers need to tread sensitively: art-making can be a very private activity – pupils simply may not wish either to be intruded upon in process, or pressured to feel they *have* to talk about it. At the same time, pupils need to learn to appreciate the comments of others, and the communicative effect and impact of their work.

With pupils with limited verbal skills, much will depend on the teacher's skilled questioning. Using *closed questions* (those that demand a yes/no answer) paradoxically may enable certain pupils to comment on a piece of work. Teachers may employ a *hierarchy of questioning*, beginning with an open question, and gradually narrowing the parameters:

What did you use to put on the paint?
Did you use a brush or a spreader?
Did you use a thick brush or a thin brush?
Did you use a thick brush – yes or no?

1 Initially, pupils may need to *consolidate the notion of cause and effect* – their power to make a statement using art tools and materials in different techniques; for example, printing purposefully with a potato, to make a series of marks. It is crucial that pupils can *see* their work, and the end result displayed, for pupils to connect the 'process' with the 'product'. Mounting work on the wall at pupils' eye level as soon as possible – even if only for the duration of the session before the pupils take their work home – will enable them to view and experience their work, and to make the connection that *they* created it. Other pupils' attention should be drawn to it, ideally in group or class discussion and 'sharing' time, with their responses invited.

2 Pupils need to be enabled to *make guided choices* in their art-making. This can be a sensitive matter (see *Art for All – The Practice,* chapter 3). Pupils with learning difficulties, in particular, may need *time* to make connections and to think through a process or technique. Staff may struggle to reconcile giving pupils the time they may need, with the pressures and constraints of a shortened day typical of a special school situation. Pupils need to be aware of options (but not too many at once) on using tools and materials, and encouraged to try out *or* reject an idea. This is important – ultimate 'ownership' of a piece of work should be the pupil's, and pupils should have the right ultimately to make an executive decision concerning their work. Supporting staff need to time their intervention sensitively, waiting for pupils to pause if working happily, and pre-empting frustration setting in if interest is waning. In this way, pupils may learn to review and modify their work in process, with the support of an interested adult.

3 Pupils may be encouraged to discuss or *comment on their work after its completion.* Beware offering comments and asking questions like 'that's nice – what is it?'. Not only may this be demoralising, but also imply that the work has to be representational, whereas an abstract piece may be perfectly valid, even if not one's personal 'cup of tea'. Teacher's questioning should probe beyond superficial content or subject matter (if it is a representational piece), to elicit from the pupils comments or utterances to do with how they created it; for example, describing images in the work, naming colours used, etc.

4 Pupils need to realise that they *have the option of returning to their work on a future occasion.* Sensitivity has to be employed in asking a pupil whether or not a piece of work is 'finished' or could be developed further. Pupils may be encouraged to comment on what might be changed or developed; for example, returning to a painting to add detail with graphic materials (see figure 5.6 p.39).

5 As pupils become habituated to standing back from their work in process, so they may be encouraged to *slow down and pause their art-making, to research solutions to 'problems' arising*. For example, pausing their work to develop and practise a particular technique, or to discover various possibilities for achieving a particular effect. Pupils may have had a clear intention at the outset; alternatively, they may have trusted to the materials, for inspiration to emerge from explorations and experiments. Either way, work may need to be paused, in order to research a further development.

6 Pupils may learn to *consider and value the comments of other people* on their work. An appropriate atmosphere and forum needs to be established, in which pupils may express their reactions to the work of their peers. Pieces of work should be given equal regard and status by the teacher, fostering the notion that everyone's art is a legitimate statement. Discussion should focus on considering approaches, techniques, tools, materials and use of the art elements, and should be sensitively 'fielded' by the teacher, to take account of any negative group dynamics. It may be preferable to invite pupils to comment *favourably* on another pupil's work initially: maybe to say or indicate something that they really like about the work. Pupils may be encouraged to offer *constructive* criticism: maybe express their reservations about something in the work of another pupil, but to support and substantiate their comments, and offer alternative ideas or possibilities. Pupils nevertheless should feel that they have the right to act on *or* to reject a suggestion for developing their work further.

CHAPTER 3

Pattern and Texture

Pattern and Texture in Art-Making

Pupils should be taught to experiment with and use pattern and texture in a range of media, in two- and three-dimensional work; also to recognise pattern and texture in the work of other artists. Pattern is simply a considered arrangement of shapes, forms, textures and colours (Lancaster, 1990). Pattern occurs in both the natural and made environment: e.g. animal skins, cross-sections of fruit and vegetables, architectural cornicing, road markings, etc. Pattern may be created on a surface in different ways: by impressing into it, embossing it, painting or drawing on it, printing onto it, etc. This may affect the surface quality – degrees of roughness and smoothness. This surface quality is known as texture. Texture may be real: for example, applying paint thickly in layers (impasto) will give a raised surface to a work. Texture may also be illusory: for example, line and tonal drawings may suggest the quality of a particular surface.

The two elements of pattern and texture may *interact* – each can give the impression of the other:

- This interaction may be *real,* with texture created from pattern. Making a pattern (random or ordered) from arranging different materials may create a flat or a raised texture: fabrics, paper and 'found' items (depending on their stiffness), may be folded, woven, arched, fringed, crumpled, pleated, layered, gathered, plaited, etc, to give a three-dimensional quality.
- The interaction between pattern and texture may be *apparent:* pattern may suggest the texture of a surface; for example, a pencil drawing of a decorated pot, with tonal shading used to indicate where patterning has caused a raised and/or impressed surface.
- Pattern may be used *representationally* to suggest a particular texture: for example, embossed papers or fabrics may evoke the surface quality of snow, water, fur, grass, etc.
- Pattern and texture (real or illusory) may also be used to fill in shapes to create an *abstract* design.
- Collage emphasises the use of pattern and texture: different materials may be selected for both their feel *and* evocative qualities. For example, using pampas

grass will give a feathery, kinetic quality to an abstract work, but if attached to the end of an image of a horse would evoke the impression of a horse's tail.

Pupils may consider the *functional and decorative uses* of pattern and texture in different cultures – certain traditional designs may be inspirational. Pupils may recreate these and make their own interpretations based on them, with growing selectivity and discrimination in different practices (painting, printing, collage, etc):

- Pupils may look at patterning and texture in everyday objects: on boxes, containers, beads, curtains, cushions, china, picture frames, etc. What kind of pattern makes for a peaceful bedroom wallpaper or an eye-catching jumper? How are pieces arranged so that they tessellate to produce a pattern in a mosaic floor or for a patchwork quilt?
- Different cultures have explored pattern in their artistic traditions, e.g.: Hindu rangoli patterns for floors and walls; Mendhi patterns on the hands and feet of Muslim women; paper cuts in Polish folk art; stencilled motifs (flowers, buds, hearts, bells, etc) of American pioneers; interlocking hearts or diamonds, or symmetrical crosses and knot designs in Irish Celtic culture, etc.
- Particular textures and patterns have been valued in various art traditions; e.g., the Aztecs prized feathers and used strong geometric designs and fretwork patterning, which may inspire their use in pupils' own work.
- Architecture provides ready-made examples of uses of pattern and texture on a large scale. For example, cathedrals provide awe-inspiring examples of designs made from circles, zig-zags, arches and crosses, and recurring motifs, in structures, embellishments and in stained glass windows.
- Certain cultures have used pattern *symbolically* – pupils may invent their own symbol system in visual patterning. For example, the Aborigines used dotted patterns to depict landscapes and concentric circles to represent a hill, stone or fire.

Developing Understanding of Pattern and Texture

Developing a sense of touch and an awareness that everything around them has its own *texture* is an integral part of pupils' sensory exploration and discovery of their world and how materials behave. This may represent a crucial underpinning for many pupils with learning difficulties: enabling them to 'recapture' early sensory experiences of the natural and made environment. Pupils need 'hands on' exploration of a range of different textures and patterns, as the foundation on which to develop their art-making (see figures 3.1 and 3.2 p.12). A range of fabrics, threads, fibres and objects or items with surfaces of different kinds (wood, metal, plastic, paper, card, etc) may be collected for pupils to sort and classify – both to feed their awareness of their different qualities, and also to develop a class resource to be used in art-making. Pupils may experiment with different ways of reproducing them: feeling surfaces and describing them, before taking rubbings, drawing them, painting them, etc. Myers (1989) describes a range of activities appropriate for pupils at differing stages of development, and indicates how manual dexterity may enhance art-making possibilities.

Pupils may explore different ways to *create random patterns and textures* of their own. These may be created for their own sake. Techniques may also be harnessed for their expressive and evocative qualities, in abstract and representational work (see figure 3.3 p.11). For example: taking a line 'for a walk' so that it interlocks with other lines; trailing lines and applying patches of glue and sprinkling with sand, salt, sugar, sawdust, glitter, etc, when dry; taking rubbings off different surfaces (e.g. hessian, tyres, plimsolls, brick, tree bark) using white paper or fabric and the side of a wax crayon; exploring malleable material (clay, dough, plasticene) by impressing and etching into it, as well as combining lumps to create a raised surface; spattering paint blobs on wet or dry paper; tracing pathways in paint using fingers, combs, toy cars; applying paint with different implements (sponges, palette knives, corrugated card, etc); squirting paint from bottles to create raised lines; blowing paint through a straw or trickling puddles of paint; thickening paint with different substances (PVA glue, sawdust, washing powder, etc); bubble printing (blowing through a straw into paint mixed with washing up liquid, then placing paper gently onto the head of bubbles); printing in paint with found sources, different body parts, etc.

Pupils may be challenged to *create patterns* of growing complexity, using both found sources and drawing implements. Recreating pattern using graphic materials (drawing and writing implements) is more challenging than arranging items or printing with materials to achieve a desired pattern or texture. Drawing or painting a pattern of irregular or regular shapes demands envisaging, and knowledge of, those desired shapes. Graphic tools may be offered to pupils as a means for designing pattern and/or creating a sense of texture *on* a surface, but also for impressing *into* a surface; for example, etching into a polystyrene tile using a ball-point pen, or into a clay surface using a modelling tool.

Pupils may be made aware of different media, and which are best suited to *create different textures*; for example, charcoal will lend itself to being smudged to suggest softness or fluffiness (see figure 3.4). Pupils may appreciate how other artists have suggested a textural quality through use of line and tone; for example, how Beatrix Potter depicted the fur of animals in her drawings. A pattern may be given a textural quality by using *textiles* in the same way as 'drawing' materials: threads and fibres may be used to create raised lines, and fabrics in various shapes may be further embellished with embroidery and applique techniques.

1 Initially, pupils may engage in *sensory exploration of materials* of all kinds – fabrics, threads, papers, surfaces (wood, clay, metal, etc), whether painted, printed, embossed, impressed, rubbed, dyed or natural. They may react positively or negatively to contrasting rough and smooth textures, or to visually or tactilely stimulating patterning – perhaps raised pattern 'in relief'. Pupils may select and place preferred samples onto a glued surface, to create *random arrangements,* with staff supporting the creative decision process as necessary (see *Art for All – The Practice*, chapter 3). Varying the shape and size of the 'support' (paper, card, board, etc), may encourage pupils to explore spatial possibilities with placement of items (fabric, paper, found sources, etc).

2 Pupils may be encouraged to collect and sort materials for texture and pattern, and *make irregular arrangements;* for example, choosing appropriate materials to affix within an area to make an abstract collage. Pupils may be

easily bewildered by a plethora of materials of different shapes, colours, sizes, textures, patterns, etc. Materials of all kinds need to be presented thoughtfully, to enable pupils to concentrate on finding order. For example, initially pupils may explore plain fabrics of similar texture, and sort them by colour. They may then sort plain fabrics from 'fancy' ones. Gradually the range may be increased, with pupils asked to sort boldly contrasting samples into respective 'like' piles. Pupils may be further challenged to sort similar samples, where they have to consider finer discrimination in patterning. They may be asked to analyse the *patterns:* how are motifs arranged? In stripes? In alternate rows? Diagonally? Randomly? How big is the pattern repeat? Materials may also be sorted for their *texture* (shiny, furry, rough, smooth, etc), with their introduction similarly paced, so that pupils' perception is increasingly challenged with finer discrimination.

3 Placing materials and/or making a range of marks to create an ordered pattern (flat and/or raised) should be paced, so that pupils are progressively challenged with their designs and colour schemes. Pupils may *make regular arrangements* from pieces of fabric or paper cut in the same geometric shape, or from the same material – do they spontaneously arrange pieces in an order, placing pieces the same way up, in a line, along radials, concentrically, etc? Pupils may find it helpful to experiment with arranging items on a background lattice of guidelines or within creases of folded paper: for example, printing with a variety of 'found' items along stripes or radials, impressing 'found' items into clay, making tessellating patterns as in a patchwork (sticking fabric or paper hexagons or triangles, rather than sewing pieces), or overlapping patches of fabric.

4 Pupils may progress to *making alternating patterns* (two- or three-dimensional) from contrasting sets of materials (fabrics, grasses, dried foods, foil dishes, etc) or by making contrasting marks (lines, dots, letter shapes, writing patterns, etc). At first, this may vary only in one aspect – by colour or shape or size; for example, little red squares and little red circles. Gradually, pupils may be further challenged, to make *repeated patterns* of increasing complexity, using materials or marks varying in two or more aspects – colour and/or shape and/or size; for example, big red squares – little blue circles – big green triangles. Pupils with learning difficulties may find it easier to deal with regular geometric shapes initially, rather than be distracted by irregular forms or representational motifs.

5 Pupils may progress to *making more complex repeated patterns,* using detailed motifs to create designs. These may be inspired by the natural environment: the way fish scales overlap; the colouring, and orientation of feathers; the arterial patterning of leaf veins; radial patterns in cross-sections of oranges; concentric circles of tree trunk cross-sections, etc. Pupils may also consider patterning in the made environment, and replicate designs in different media: boldly contrasting designs on fabrics, wallpaper, china, ornaments, etc; symmetrical striped design on a tea towel; a geometric pattern on a jumper; concentric circles on the rim of a plate, etc.

6 Pupils may consider the *use of pattern and texture for a particular purpose* and for their expressive qualities, and select materials to suggest features or to create a particular effect, with attention to choice of colour and negative as

well as positive shapes (spaces between motifs). For example: combining collage with paint to create an abstract picture in the style of Cubist artists such as Picasso or Braque; designing a series of wall tiles based on the work of Morgan; making a thematic collage based on a photograph, selecting materials (fabrics, threads, paper, etc) of particular colours (naturalistic or abstract), patterns and textures to suggest features and details. Pupils may be challenged to create *abstract designs with increasingly complex patterns*, in a range of media: paisley-patterns, intricate mosaics, whorls and loops, Rangoli patterns, etc. They may progress to exploring 'exploded' shapes (cut up geometric shapes or silhouettes of familiar objects or creatures) with the pieces arranged slightly apart; quilling patterns (from rolled and coiled paper strips); arranging motifs within grids or segments of circles; using compasses and ruler to make concentric circles and regular geometric designs, and filling spaces with collage materials (lentils, seeds, buttons, sequins, etc); arranging rubbings in a pattern or design.

Using Pattern and Texture

Inspiring pattern and texture

The patterning or texture of a particular sample of fabric may remind pupils of something in their environment; this may be used as a *starting-point for picture-making*, maybe using mixed media, such as adding pencil or felt pen to complete an image. Pupils may make a design based on patterns used to notate a composition graphically in music: a range of marks linked to beats or when particular instruments play (e.g. pre-writing patterns: olol olol olol). Pupils may also generate abstract patterns, by drawing or painting to music with contrasting and repeated sections: changing their marks to reflect changes in the pattern of the music (e.g. staccato – legato – staccato).

Pupils with learning difficulties will need plenty of *reference material* (real objects and photographs) to inform pattern-making and the creation of textures in their own work. They need to pick out distinguishing features and particular areas of surface decoration or texture, then select from an appropriately structured range of materials, or work in mixed media, to recreate an effect. For example, pupils may work from black and white photographs, or images enlarged on the photocopier (see *Art for All – The Practice*, figures 6.4 and 6.5), and experiment with fabrics and papers in a limited colour range (not necessarily monochrome), to explore the use of texture and pattern to recreate images and tonal effects (e.g. brickwork).

Pupils may consider how *different artists have used pattern and texture* in a range of materials, techniques and media; for example, the way various artists have suggested the texture of tree trunks in two- and three-dimensional work, or used samples of real bark for its evocative quality (abstract or representational) – the Aborigines painted on bark. Certain artists have also used pattern symbolically, or favoured certain motifs; pupils may make their own designs, inspired by their work. For example, Klimt's arrangements of geometric shapes in certain colour combinations: circles to represent femininity, and oblongs for masculinity. The images in the work of developmentally young children, characteristically appear 'flat' and unrounded. This is because young children tend not to use shading in their work, which would give the impression of volume to objects, and a sense of depth. Many artists have deliberately harnessed this, and *played down* a sense of depth and three-dimensional quality by flattening their images, to achieve the effect of bringing surface details and decoration, patterning and spatial arrangements of images into prominence. This is a challenging concept, let alone for pupils with learning difficulties. However, they may be able to consider how artists such as Matisse, Lowry, Klee and Klimt have exploited this in their work.

Creating designs

Pupils may be inspired by patterning or textures in their environment to *create their own designs*. These may be simple or complex, random or ordered, depending on the ability of the pupil. Random patterns of geometric shapes (painted, printed or stencilled directly onto a plain fabric) may be within the grasp of many pupils. Pupils should be challenged to create a design according to their ability to follow a sequence, their hand-eye co-ordination, and their ability to make an ordered arrangement. Pupils may create an original design based on motifs drawn from a texture in the natural or made environment. They may consider commercial samples derived in this way, before contemplating their own source of inspiration. Pupils may work through a 'design process' (based on Holder and Coleman, 1994):

- *Considering a selected object from different perspectives:* in outline, in cross-section and from different angles, and noting colours. Pupils may record their observations by drawing, cutting and tearing paper shapes, taking photographs, placing it on the photocopier, etc.
- *Working out a range of possible designs* in rough on paper. Pupils should think of an outline or a particular texture as a *starting-point,* and select and edit it as they wish. They should be encouraged to simplify the image, not be distracted by detail. For example, outlines may be used as a template to be drawn round or as the basis for a stencil or for a printing 'block', and replicated in a repeated pattern.
- *Selecting the most viable design,* with consideration of colour, shape and spatial arrangement of motifs: e.g. in vertical, horizontal or diagonal patterns; size of pattern, repeat, etc.
- *Revising the design;* for example: the size of the design – will it transfer directly, or will it need to be scaled up or down? Adapting the design to fit a particular space – will it need to be squashed? Elongated? Considering the design in the light of the intended technique for applying it onto fabric – will it need to be simplified or elaborated?
- *Making a finished product* by applying the design to the fabric. Pupils may have a particular technique in mind, with which to create their design. Alternatively, the teacher may have a particular method in mind, to which pupils may need to adapt their designs accordingly. Pupils may be aware of tools and materials required, and also consider the amount of time they may need.
- *Reviewing their work* and considering what amendments they would make next time. For example, the suitability of their design for a particular purpose (T-shirt, cushion cover, curtain, etc), and whether it needs adapting or modifying (e.g. choice of colours to fit a particular context, such as a bedroom colour scheme).

Figure 3.4 *'Leopard' (charcoal drawing by senior pupil with severe learning difficulties). This pupil has explored possibilities for suggesting patterning and textural qualities of his subject, by smudging and fluffing the charcoal, as well as using the edge and side of the stick to create lines and tones.*

Textiles in art-making

Using fabrics and threads offers many opportunities for pupils to work in two and three dimensions, and inherently emphasises the elements of texture and pattern. Many pupils with learning difficulties will struggle to become proficient in using a needle and thread. However, there are many ways of using fabrics and threads which do not entail needlework. Fabrics are flexible and reasonably resilient, and can be manipulated – folded, twisted, pleated, pulled, etc. When combined with adhesive by soaking in paste or PVA, or with structures made from wire, wood, cane, etc, they may be used to create three-dimensional forms. They may also be embellished with threads, stitches, beads, fabric pieces stuck on, etc. Pupils may find it easier to work on fabrics pulled taut; for example, held in a traditional circular wooden frame, or taped over a board or work surface.

Early experiences of textiles will entail *multi-sensory exploration* of their different qualities: feeling, pulling, twisting, smoothing, crumpling, smelling them, holding them up to the light, listening to their different sounds, etc. Pupils may be encouraged to find descriptive words, and to sort and classify fabrics, yarns and threads in different ways (see above). Fabrics may be investigated and examined, perhaps using a magnifying glass, to ascertain how they were made (bonded, knitted or woven), what they feel like, whether they are strong, waterproof, warm, etc; and what they might be used for.

Pupils may explore *making textiles* – constructing them by spinning, knitting, weaving, crochet, knotting and making felt. A pattern may be built into the construction, although this may be difficult for many pupils with learning difficulties to follow. Pupils may be challenged to recreate the texture of different fabrics using other media (pencil, pastels, felt pen, ball-point pen, etc). They may examine how yarns are made: plaited, twisted, etc; and learn techniques of combining strands to make a new thicker, single strand.

Fabrics may be used to *give a textural and/or three-dimensional quality* to two-dimensional work. For example: abstract collages from cut, torn or fringed fabrics; contributing 'real' highlights to a representational image (e.g. adding a real bow made from a piece of ribbon to a painting of a figure); soaking fabric in glue and scrunching or moulding it in place to make an image 'in relief'; using wadding or padding (crumpled paper, cotton wool, etc) overlain with fabric and glued into place or stitched in applique techniques or quilting. Rather than (or as well as) acquiring a repertoire of conventional embroidery stitches, certain pupils may learn to 'draw' with 'free' stitching or stuck lengths of yarn or thread (this may be fiddly), and experiment with loosely and densely hatched and cross-hatched areas to suggest 'shading' (refer to figure 5.3).

Fabrics and threads may be *woven,* perhaps linked to an evocative theme (e.g. the sea-side, jungle, etc), using different materials in a limited range of colours. A wide range of materials may be woven – string, strips of paper or plastic, ribbon, braid, grasses, etc. Certain pupils with learning difficulties may find this a challenging technique. Careful consideration should be given to the type of materials: sturdy ones initially, and on a large enough scale for pupils to grasp the principle (e.g. a bicycle wheel as a loom, or garden canes or sticks tied together), progressing to 'looms' demanding greater dexterity. Certain pupils may find looms with string or yarn warp challenging. They may be able to cope better with weaving through mesh (e.g. plastic garden netting or trellis, chicken wire, onion sacks, sequin band, etc). Pupils may try weaving strips of paper in a range of widths through slit card, polystyrene meat packaging dishes, or paper (including pre-painted or printed) to make a 'mat'. They may experiment with irregular free weaving at first (loose over-under patterns), then weaving over-one under-one, progressing to weaving with two colours and different patterns – e.g. over-one, under-two, and so on. Weaving threads using a needle through loosely woven fabrics (netting, lace, crochet, knitting, hessian, binca, etc), may help pupils to understand principles and refine their skills for sewing 'over and under' using a needle.

Fabrics may be coloured and/or embellished, to create random and/or regular patterning. Patterns may be drawn, painted or printed (using found sources, sponges, brushes, etc) onto fabrics using wax crayons (cover with paper and iron to make permanent), fabric paints, ordinary paints or inks (if they are not to be washed). 'Resist' patterns on fabrics may be made by using card stencils or sticking on adhesive labels, masking or parcel tape, then applying paint or dye; silk screen printing is based on a stencil principle, and is within the grasp of many pupils with learning difficulties. 'Negative' patterning may also be created in techniques of *batik* (drawing with hot wax using a tjanting tool, to repel colour), and *tie-dye* (gathering and knotting fabrics with string or elastic bands, then dipping in dye and removing binds when dry, to leave concentric and radiating uncoloured areas). Pupils may make their own dyes for fabrics and yarns from plants, fruit and vegetables (e.g. blackberries – pink, onion skin – yellow, red cabbage – blue, coffee – brown).

CHAPTER 4

Colour

Colour in Art-Making

Everything has a colour, even if it is black and white. Colours vary in their intensity: a hue (name of a colour – e.g. red, blue or yellow) may appear bright (strong intensity) or dull (low intensity), or somewhere in between. Colour is used selectively by artists for its evocative qualities, its emotional impact and sometimes its symbolic significance (for example, colour in Medieval art). Reactions to colour vary between cultures and between historical times: associations of particular colours can be hard to break, as we are socialised into them. For example, in contemporary western society, red is associated with warmth and passion and is used to suggest a warning (traffic lights, hot taps, etc); however in China, red is connected with marriage. In contemporary western culture, blue is commonly associated with coldness or remoteness, whereas in Renaissance times, blue was used to signify virginity and purity in paintings of the Madonna.

In the Renaissance, a strong hierarchy of appropriate subject matter for paintings was established, which upheld the importance of 'storytelling': the depiction of naturalistic scenes from classical mythology or the Bible. This supremacy became displaced in the nineteenth century, with a growing interest in landscape and nature; for example, the work of Constable, Gainsborough, etc. Monet, Cezanne and Matisse used these themes to challenge approaches to painting, to express a mood or an idea. They showed how colour could have an expressive purpose of its own, rather than be used to fill in areas made by lines and shapes. This resulted in the 'emancipation of colour', such that many western artists have explored colour for its own sake in the late nineteenth and twentieth centuries; for example, the contemporary British artists, Bridget Riley and Patrick Heron.

Pupils may be offered experiences with colour for its own sake, although it is all-too-easy to become carried away with presenting pupils with a bombardment of visual stimulation in ad hoc activities. Many teachers are familiar with activities such as marbling, tissue paper collage, making melted wax crayon prints, weaving coloured paper, yarns or fabrics, etching into wax crayon or oil pastel scraperboards, spattering paint on wet or dry paper and spraying with a plant mister, etc. However, pupils need to become aware of the range of colours available, and learn how these may be created, combined, and how they may interact with one another, so that they may use colour to realise a particular intention in their art-making. This may be achieved *gradually*, through pupils working with a *limited* range of colours over which they may increasingly develop more control and awareness, with growing sensitivity and selectivity.

Understanding colour theory in a way that they will subsequently be able to articulate will be beyond many pupils with learning difficulties. However, the *teacher* needs to have some grasp of the behaviour of colours in order to structure learning opportunities for the pupils: to enable them to make connections as far as possible, and gradually to acquire control over selecting and creating the colours they require. In order for pupils to learn about colour, teachers need to return to first principles, and build up their knowledge gradually, if necessary, as co-learners alongside the pupils.

Art materials will offer varying potential for making new colours or optical effects, depending on whether they are to be used 'wet' or 'dry' (see *Art for All – The Practice*, chapters 5 and 6). New colours may be created in various ways; for example, by combining colours in a 'wet' medium (paint, ink, fabric dyes, etc), by overlaying translucent materials (tissue paper, coloured acetate, chiffon fabric, etc), or by laying patches or streaks of colour in juxtaposition using 'dry' materials (coloured pencils, chalks, oil pastels, etc). The intensity of a colour may be weakened or strengthened by adjusting the degree of dilution in 'wet' materials, or the amount of pressure exerted with 'dry' materials; this will create tonal contrasts. Understanding how optical effects may be created using 'wet' and/or 'dry' materials, will be dependent on a solid grasp of the behaviour of colour; this will be learned essentially through opportunities to work in *paint*. For example, the knowledge that placing felt pen dots of red and blue in juxtaposition will create a new colour ('mixed in the eye' when viewed from a distance) will be founded in an understanding of how purple may be mixed from red and blue paint.

Developing Understanding of Colour

Primary colours (red, yellow and blue) cannot be mixed from any other colour – all other colours can actually be created from using them in combination, with the addition of white and black. For the purposes of educating pupils about colour, greater quantities of the primary colours and white will be needed. Pupils will acquire more control and understanding of the behaviour of colour by working initially with a *restricted* range. Experiences using paint will be fundamental, offering the fluidity required for experimenting with colour. Early discoveries may be made most easily 'on the paper' (see figure 4.1 p.37). Pupils may gradually become aware of broad colour correlations in their environment (see figure 6.2 p.40). In time, pupils may learn how to use a mixing palette to create greater subtlety of a colour they may require (see figure 4.2 p.38).

Pupils with learning difficulties should work towards being able to control and use colour from as broad a 'palette' as possible. It will be the teacher's responsibility to structure opportunities for developing pupils' understanding and use of colour, by presenting an appropriate range from which new colours may be created. Pupils should be confident in handling a particular combination of colours before proceeding to a new combination. Experiences of a particular combination may need repeating many times. Pupils require this familiarity in order to develop their confidence, and to consolidate their knowledge and understanding sufficiently to be able to replicate producing a particular colour on a future occasion. At the same time, pupils should also have variety and breadth: discovering possibilities through combining other colours in a similar manner; e.g. creating a range of greens from different blues and yellows. This may all seem very complicated, but principles of mixing and using colour can be acquired step by step, over many years.

1 Pupils may be offered *experiences with a range of colours* in different media, although not too dazzling an array at any one time, as this will be bewildering. Pupils may be asked to sort and match a selection of fabrics, papers, etc. They may be challenged gradually to match samples with increasingly finer distinctions between shades and tints; e.g. sorting tissue paper pieces in a range of reds and pinks prior to a collage activity. In drawing and painting, they may be offered opportunities to explore mark-making using one colour at a time. Pupils may well be more interested in their marks rather than the colour itself, although they may be encouraged to select and name a required colour. Marks need to be seen clearly, and should contrast with the background colour of the 'support' (paper, card, etc) – white is best for colour experiments. Pupils may begin to discover the behaviour of colour: for example, painting in a primary colour (red, blue or yellow), with white added a drop at a time, and/or drops of a second primary colour, for pupils to 'poke' at and discover the effect of the colours mixing (see figure 4.1 p.37). Working on wet paper, or spraying paint with a plant mister, will cause it to run and blur, and create areas of strong and faint colour.

2 Pupils may be taught to *make colours lighter and/or darker,* by gradually adding dark to light, a small amount at a time. The *tone* of the colour (its lightness or darkness) will be affected by the addition of black (or blue) to make *shades,* and/or white to create *tints.* Black is potentially disastrous! Only a tiny amount is needed for darkening colours – the Impressionist artists dispensed with black, and created shades by adding blue instead. In representational work, pupils may not be bothered which colour they use to draw or paint (e.g. a tree). The teacher may feel anxious to impose a more accurate colour match; however, the teacher may not have that same concern if the child happens to be using a pencil, with everything depicted in shades of grey. The point is that in the eyes of the pupil it is the images that are important, with the actual colour of secondary significance. Nevertheless, pupils' experience and understanding of the behaviour of colour needs to be broadened, with developing control over creating tints and shades.

3 Pupils' awareness of broad colour relations in their environment may be emerging (e.g. blue for sky, green for grass, etc). They may learn to select colours which, when mixed, will *make a new secondary colour,* with its

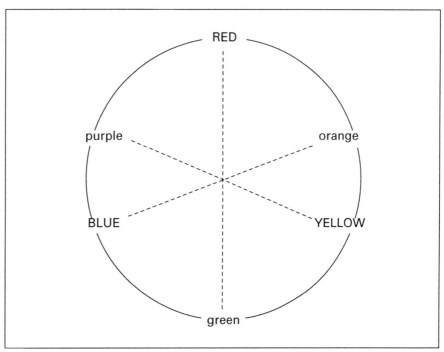

Figure 4.3: *The relationship of primary and secondary colours.*

corresponding range of tints and shades by adding white or black. Artists often refer to a colour wheel – figure 4.3 illustrates the relationship between the primary colours (in capitals) which cannot be mixed from any other colour, and the secondary colours (in lower case) that are created from mixing the two primary colours on either side.

4 Pupils may acquire a growing awareness of subtleties of colour in their environment. Pupils may be challenged to *mix a range of secondary colours, with associated shades and tints.* There are 'hot' and 'cold' versions of each of the primary colours. The commonest versions of the 'hot' primary colours in schools are called 'brilliant'; specialist artists' materials may refer to them as (e.g.) cadmium red or vermillion, cadmium yellow and ultramarine.

'hot'	*'cold'*
brilliant red	crimson
brilliant blue	cobalt blue
brilliant yellow	lemon yellow

Versions of primary colours will tend to have a bias towards the secondary colour adjacent to them on the colour wheel. However, the truest or *pure primary* colour may be achieved by mixing the 'hot' and 'cold' versions of the same hue; for example, a pillar box red may be made from mixing brilliant red (vermillion) with crimson. Figure 4.4 illustrates the relationship of the 'hot' and 'cold' primaries on the colour wheel to the secondary colours (in capitals). Combinations of 'hot' and 'cold' primaries will affect the secondary colour when mixed. Those truest or *pure secondary* colours will be created from mixing the two primaries nearest to them on the colour wheel:

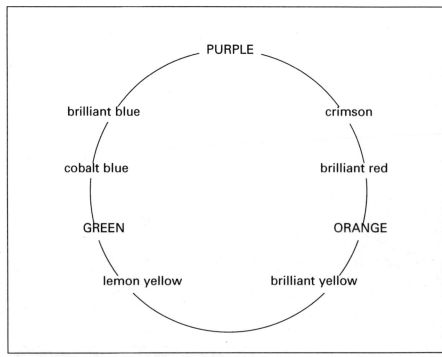

Figure 4.4: *The relationship of 'hot' and 'cold' primary colours and pure secondary colours.*

brilliant red	+	brilliant yellow	=	orange
crimson	+	brilliant blue	=	purple
cobalt blue	+	lemon yellow	=	green

As well as mixing vibrant, pure secondary colours, pupils may learn to mix a range of oranges, purples and greens of different intensities, from mixing various permutations of primary colours. These are known as *muted secondaries* – for example, an olive green from brilliant yellow and brilliant blue. Muted colours can be used to produce subtle contrasts and a sense of harmony (see figure 4.5 p.38). Adding white or black to the combinations will increase the range of possible tints and shades. Consider the following secondary colours created from mixing 'hot' and 'cold' primaries (* indicates the 'pure' secondary in each group):

brilliant red*	+	brilliant yellow	
crimson	+	brilliant yellow	ORANGES
brilliant red	+	lemon yellow	
crimson	+	lemon yellow	
brilliant blue*	+	crimson	
cobalt blue	+	crimson	PURPLES
brilliant blue	+	brilliant red	
cobalt blue	+	brilliant red	
lemon yellow*	+	cobalt blue	
brilliant yellow	+	cobalt blue	GREENS
lemon yellow	+	brilliant blue	
brilliant yellow	+	brilliant blue	

Figure 4.1: *Discovering orange (abstract painting in brilliant red, brilliant yellow and white, by nursery pupil with severe learning difficulties). The fluidity of the paint has enabled 'accidental' discoveries to be made on the paper*

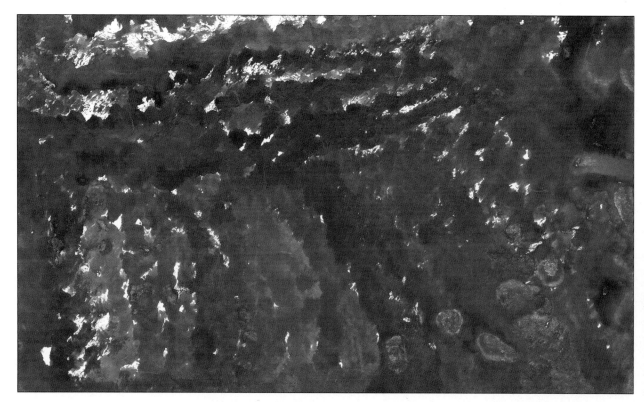

Figure 4.2: *Abstract painting, inspired by Monet's 'Soleil Levant' (by senior pupil with severe learning difficulties). This pupil chose to explore Monet's limited palette, to experiment with creating shades and tints of reds and purples. He used brilliant red, crimson, brilliant blue and cobalt blue and white; the result has a harmonious quality.*

Figure 4.5: *'War sky' (painting in muted secondary colours, by senior pupil with severe learning difficulties). This pupil has deliberately mixed sludgy colours to evoke his chosen theme.*

38

Figure 5.6: 'A plane crashes in the nasty war (painting and oil pastel by senior pupil with severe learning difficulties). This work is by the same pupil as figure 3.4. Here, he has rejected line and tone, to create an abstract interpretation of his subject that uses irregular shapes in patches of bright colour, carefully placed over the support.*

Figure 5.2 *Landscape inspired by Turner (oil pastel drawing by senior pupil with severe learning difficulties). This girl has experimented with techniques used by Turner, to suggest areas of light and dark: placing a very dark tree against an area of intensely light sky; also blending shades and creating tints directly on the support (here, by layering and smudging black and white with other hues).*

Figure 6.2: *'Duck' (felt pen drawing by junior pupil with moderate learning difficulties). This girl has used felt pens as a colouring agent to fill in areas, also to make line drawings, to suggest outlines and contours. Her work shows a clear sense of ordering images.*

5 *Pupils may learn about complementary colours and how to mix tertiary colours.*
The primary colour not involved in creating the secondary colour, is known
as its *complementary colour.* For example, purple is made from combining red
and blue; its complementary colour therefore is yellow (see figure 4.3).
Shades and tints of primary colours will also have complementary partners;
for example, light green and maroon. Artists exploit complementary pairs in
their handling of colour (see below – Using Colour).

primary combinations			*secondary colour*	*complementary colour*
red	+	blue	= purple	: yellow
yellow	+	blue	= green	: red
red	+	yellow	= orange	: blue

By adjusting proportions of primary and secondary colours adjacent to
each other on the colour wheel, it is possible to produce a range of
tertiary colours, from secondary colours with a bias towards the primary
colour nearest to it. Mixing complementary pairs of colours will
neutralise them, and produce a subtle range of greys and browns,
containing varying proportions of red, blue and yellow. The range of
tertiary colours will be further expanded by mixing them with white
and/or black, to create tints and shades. Figure 4.6 illustrates the 'tertiary'
colours (in bold) on the colour wheel, with the 'pure' secondary colours
in capitals:

6 Pupils may learn to *mix and use colour for its expressive and evocative
qualities.* They may develop awareness of the behaviour of colours in
relation to one another, and understanding of their effect on the viewer;
for example, harmonising and discordant colour (see figure 4.2 p.38, also
figure 5.6 p.39), and the 'temperature' of colours (see below). Pupils may
progress to learning to mix colour to a required intensity, with an
awareness of the surface to be worked on; for example, thickening
powder paint prior to applying to coloured sugar paper background;
applying oil pastels with varying pressure to achieve a desired colour
intensity.

Using Colour

Colours can be placed strategically and/or in juxtaposition, in order to create
a particular effect (based on Smith, 1994).

Temperature of colour

Colours are often described as being 'hot' or 'cold': 'hot' colours are reds, yellow
and oranges; 'cold' colours are blues, greens and purples. 'Hot' colours seem to
advance towards the viewer, whilst 'cold' colours seem to recede. Interior
designers exploit this effect in creating illusions of space – for example, a small
area can seem larger if painted in cool blue. Artists explore this apparent physical
behaviour of colour in the composition of a work – for example, creating the
effect of space and a sense of depth, by depicting distant hills in a landscape in
shades of blue. Velasquez often strengthened warm flesh pinks by placing them
next to areas of cool blue and grey.

Complementary colours

Selective placement of complementary partners causes colour to behave in certain ways:

- When complementary colours are placed next to each other, they tend to create the optical effect of emphasising each other's intensity; for example, red and green together will make each other more vibrant – Constable put touches of red amongst green areas in his landscapes.
- A splash of colour amongst a patch of its complementary partner can be used to draw the eye as a focal point.
- Using a secondary colour can make a lively shadow for an object in its complementary primary – for example, painting a purple shadow for a yellow ball, a technique much explored by Van Gogh.
- An over dominant, strident colour can be toned down by adding a little of its complementary partner.
- Mixing complementary partners will produce a range of subtle greys and browns, containing proportions of red, yellow and blue; adding white or black will increase the range of tints and shades.
- Optical mixing on the paper or canvas can be created by placing patches of dots of complementary colours in juxtaposition; from a distance, this will create a new colour – the Impressionist painters exploited this technique, and it was developed to an extreme in the 'pointilliste' work of the Post-Impressionist painter, Seurat.

Harmonising colour

Colours may be used in *harmony* to create a sense of cohesion and mood. If the teacher structures an activity, such that colours will intrinsically harmonise in a pupils' paintings, this may help create a positive response and satisfying reaction from the pupils to their work, as well as from prospective viewers. It will also enable a display of pupils' individual work to link together, and maybe create a useful background mood or foil – for example, shades of blue to create a 'cold' backdrop for a classroom environment reflecting a topic on 'Winter'. Pupils may be taught to appreciate how artists have used colour in different ways to achieve a harmonising, unifying effect, and try out similar methods in their own work. The teacher needs to be aware of different ways in which harmony may be achieved, as:

- restricting the choice of colours available to those close together in the colour wheel; e.g. works in Picasso's 'blue' phase;
- working in 'hot' colours, 'cold' colours, or neutrals; e.g. Gwen John's work in muted colours;
- using the tone of the underlying paper or an undercoat ('ground') of paint, which may integrate with the colour applied over it; e.g. Degas' choice of paper in mid-tones for his pastel drawings;
- using colours adjacent in the colour wheel that share a common primary colour; e.g. Van Gogh's use of yellows and oranges to create his famous 'Sunflowers';
- using a range of colours of the same hue; e.g. seascapes in shades of blue;
- using two sets of harmonies in the same work; e.g. shades of yellows to

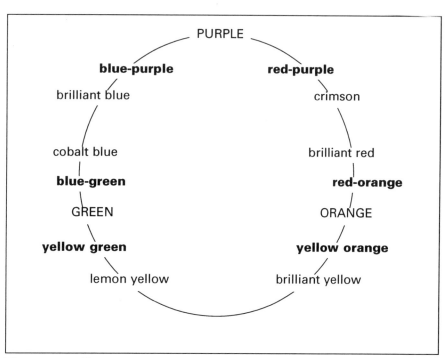

Figure 4.6: *The relationship of primary, secondary and tertiary colours.*

depict a sunny sky, and shades of purple to depict shadows cast on mountains.

Discordant colour

Clashing or *discordant colours* can be used deliberately to have a jarring, unsettling effect. The teacher should be aware of the potential impact on both the pupil and ultimately the viewer, of the range of materials offered. Harmonising pictures by pupils, potentially, can be spoilt if the teacher unwittingly selects a clashing backing paper on which to mount a display. Offering pupils a random array of paints may prevent pupils from understanding how colours can behave, as well as risking the end product resulting in something aesthetically displeasing both to the child and to the viewer. Used selectively however, it is possible to use discordant colours to create exciting effects and to draw the viewer's attention to focal points of interest. Pupils may be taught to appreciate how artists have used disconcerting colours to advantage (for example, the work of the Fauvist artists such as Derain, Matisse and Vlaminck), and try out methods and approaches in their own work, as:

- using 'hot' and 'cold' versions of the same primary colour in juxtaposition – for example, crimson clashing with brilliant red; e.g. in the work of Bonnard;
- exploiting tension between colours that 'advance' and 'recede', to make colours apparently vibrate; e.g. red and blue vertical stripes and roving lines, as in the 'op art' of Bridget Riley;
- using blocks of complementary pairs of colours on a large scale, or patches of complementary colours; e.g. Rothko's large canvases, and the work of Gauguin;

- using colour arrangements that do not appear in real life; e.g. the work of the Fauves or Expressionists;
- using colour to flatten an image by depicting background details in strong colours to bring them forward, rather than creating a sense of depth with muted colours that recede; e.g. in the work of Gauguin;
- using strong outlines and shapes; e.g. in the work of Van Gogh.

CHAPTER 5

Line and Tone

Line and Tone in Art-Making

The elements of line and tone are fundamental to two-dimensional art-making and the use of graphic materials. Line and tone also contribute to the creation and understanding of shape, and expression in three-dimensional form, and for creating pattern and texture. Children develop a repertoire of *lines* of different lengths relatively early, which they learn to enclose to make shapes and combine to make images of different sizes (see figure 5.1): verticals, horizontals, diagonals, dots, dashes, curves, waves and zig-zags. Developmentally young children commonly tend to be more preoccupied with their use of line – tone may be relatively meaningless to them, and it would be inappropriate, therefore, for the teacher to attempt to impose this awareness.

Tones are shades of light and dark – everything has a tone, as evidenced more clearly in black and white photographs, whereas to everyday view colour, pattern and texture often distract. Presenting pupils with monochrome photographs, or coloured images reproduced on a black and white photocopier, may help pupils to understand variations in tone (see *Art for All – The Practice*, figures 6.4 and 6.5). Pupils may be made aware of how other artists have used line and tone (see figure 5.2 p.40); for example, Monet depicted starkly contrasting areas of shadow and bright sunlight by adjusting tones of colour, without necessarily featuring the sun in his paintings at all.

As children become more aware of expressing the solidity of an image, they may appreciate how artists suggest a three-dimensional quality to images that are essentially two-dimensional, through the use of patches of tone to create areas of relative light and dark suggestive of shadow, and to give the impression of solidity to rounded and angular surfaces. They may consider tonal work in shades of one hue, such as blue Delftware or the Willow Pattern plate. They may consider how artists have used tones of colour also in abstract work, to create a sense of depth and three-dimensionality. For example, Malevich experimented with different shades of yellow and red geometric shapes, to make them apparently 'advance' and 'recede' (see chapter 4).

Pupils may consider how certain artists used lines compacted to different densities to suggest light and dark: perfect, regular hatching and cross-hatching of lines to different intensities and densities can become highly skilled and technically challenging, as in the work of Escher. They may also consider how artists have used lines of different lengths and densities to create a sense of texture and volume; for example, Durer's etchings, and his celebrated work 'The Young Hare'.

If pupils are to experiment with line and tone, they need to have opportunities to experience contrasts in *lighting*. This will help them to appreciate how subjects they may wish to interpret in their art-making may be lit (e.g. whether in highlight or silhouette), and how mood can be created. Working out of doors presents particular challenges in respect of lighting, with variations depending on the time of day, the season, weather and climate. Pupils may be made aware of such influences on the work of certain artists; for example, brilliant tones in strong sunlight (as in Gauguin's paintings in Tahiti), compared to softer muted colours in the landscapes of British artists like Constable and Gainsborough.

It is possible to have greater control over lighting when working indoors. Pupils may consider how different artists have worked at different times of the day, and created effects with light sources. It may be possible for pupils to experiment with recreating some of the effects, especially if there is the option of a blackout. This will help them to 'read' works by different artists, even if the subtleties of tonal discrimination are challenging for them to recreate in their own work. For example:

- natural light shafting through a window (possibly filtered with a curtain);
- firelight or candlelight (giving a glowing intensity with areas highlighted);
- lighting from the side (starkly contrasting highlight and shadow);
- lighting from underneath (underside illuminated, with shadow behind);
- adjusting the lighting to create silhouettes, contrasted with negative spaces (areas between images).

Figure 5.1 *Enclosing and combining lines to create shapes (pencil and felt pen drawing by junior pupil with severe learning difficulties). Circles with radiating lines appear in children's art across many different cultures.*

Developing Understanding of Line and Tone

Pupils may learn to make a range of increasingly purposeful marks and varied lines in a range of graphic materials: felt pens, paint, chalk, pencils, crayon, thick charcoal, fingers, ball-point pen, etc, and by impressing and etching into malleable materials such as a clay tile using a modelling tool.

1 Initially, pupils may engage in *random mark-making*, achieved by banging implements onto a surface. Pupils should be encouraged to look at their work, to establish a sense of 'cause-effect', and to develop more purposeful 'grasp-and-push' action with implements. The child may engage in increasingly *controlled scribbling*, with roving continuous lines contained within an area (see figure 4.1 p.37).

2 As control develops 'down the arm', so a greater variation of lines and marks will be possible: from large shoulder movements, to elbow then wrist action, and palmar then pincer grip of implements. Children may progress to *enclosing lines* to create an 'edge' to make a range of discrete marks, which may be placed selectively over the support. Pupils may begin to *combine lines* (close together, overlapping, inside or around each other) to produce diagrammatic shapes, such as the mandala or radial sun – a circle with spikes radiating from it (see figure 5.1). Children may (or may not) *name their scribbling*, as being about someone or something (eg 'Mummy', 'running', etc). This is a huge conceptual leap: that marks may be used representationally.

3 Children may develop their use of lines of different lengths and directions in combination, to *make images with developing control and attention to detail.* For example, the development of humanoid images may follow a characteristic progression:

  – 'big head' with marks for features (mouth, eyes, nose, ears, hair) – see figure 1.1;

  – head with limbs directly protruding (arms and/or legs) – see figure 7.2 (p.67);

  – head with torso and limbs – see figure 6.4;

  – figure with body larger than head, and including some significant details (hands, fingers, feet, toes, navel, neck, sex characteristics, etc) and clothing, suggesting volume and occasionally in profile – see figure 1.3;

  – figure with observed characteristics (beard, spectacles, moles, etc), posture, perspective, facial expression and sense of movement – see *Art for All – The Practice,* figure 5.3.

4 Pupils may learn to *use a range of lines in different thicknesses and pressures, to make outlines and details of images*, in large and small-scale work; e.g. patterning and decoration on objects or clothing; drawing an intricate motif for an abstract pattern. Versatile use of line for creating representational and abstract images, demands control of a range of lines of different qualities using the same medium (see figure 5.3). A range of lines may be made using a pencil by: varying thicknesses (using the point and/or the side of the lead); varying intensities (adjusting the pressure with which it is applied;) varying lengths (flowing, broken, swirls or dots); varying directions (curved, vertical, horizontal, diagonal).

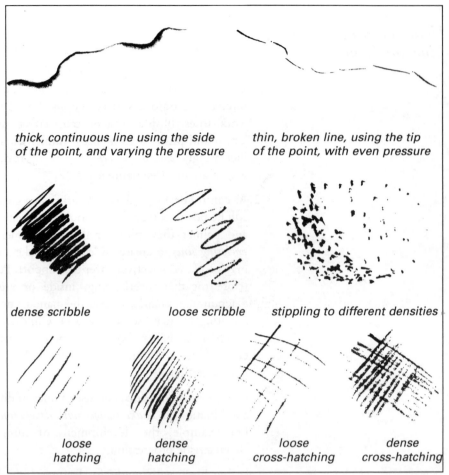

Figure 5.3 *A range of lines using pencil*

5 Pupils may be challenged to *indicate crude areas of light and dark* in their work, using a range of media. For example, using the side of a piece of charcoal to suggest the shadow of an object. Pupils may also learn how to dilute fluid materials (paint, inks, dyes, etc) to create a tonal range (see figure 5.4).

6 Pupils may learn *to use different forms of shading and cross-hatching to suggest three-dimensional quality*: volume, the contours of surfaces, light and shadow and also the texture of something. Pupils may be challenged to experiment with producing areas of darkness from lines drawn close together, and areas of relative lightness by drawing lines more loosely spaced (see figure 5.5). These may be 'scribbled', working backwards and forwards, keeping contact with the surface, or 'hatched' using crisp, separate strokes of even length in the same direction. Lines may be straight or curved, to reflect the outline and contour of an object. Spontaneous fast scribbling, or using roughly hatched and cross-hatched lines to indicate areas of light and shade, and to suggest texture, can be very effective (as in Toulouse-Lautrec's sketches of Parisian night-life); pupils may experiment with these techniques.

Using Line and Tone

Choice of medium

When selecting a medium for producing tonal images, it is important to consider the nature of the images to be reproduced, and the kind of subtlety

48

Figure 5.4 *'Two men in a boat' (Chinese brush and ink work by senior pupil with moderate learning difficulties). This girl has ground her own ink from an inkblock and diluted it to different amounts, to create a tonal range, which she has used to suggest images that are close-to, and those that are more distant.*

Figure 5.5 *'Courgettes' (pencil drawing by senior pupil with severe learning difficulties). This line drawing has areas of loose scribble applied with varying pressure, to suggest the tonality and also the patterning and texture of the subject.*

that may be required from shaded areas: whether they possess soft or hard surfaces, whether they are heavy or light, solid or hollow. Some media will not offer the sensitivity of pencil or charcoal (see figure 3.4); for example, felt pens have more limited potential for indicating a range of tones, although it may be possible to use them to create lines of different thicknesses (see figure 6.2 p.40).

Controlling media to produce a tonal range is challenging for many pupils (and adults!), let alone those with learning difficulties – for example, being able to shade to different degrees of intensity. Rounded surfaces of objects will tend to have a gradual transition between light and dark areas; angular surfaces will have more abrupt transitions. When working from first hand observation, pupils may find it easier at first to work from angular objects, to notice sharply contrasting areas of light and shade. They may progress to creating a more subtle transition of tone, to reproduce areas of relative light and dark, on curved surfaces.

If pupils are attempting to produce a tonal range or drawing of their own, it may be easier to shade all the darkest areas first, then the mid-tones and finally the lightest areas (or the other way round!); in this way, they are more likely to be able to have more uniform control. The tonal difference between images may need to be exaggerated to make it more marked. Objects shaded more densely will have a darker colour than lighter ones (check shades of grey in a black and white photograph of coloured objects).

Selecting and editing

Developmentally young children automatically edit their work, and prioritise images that have most significance to them. As pupils become more preoccupied with attention to detail, paradoxically they may have to *unlearn* this in order to assist them in recreating the images they desire. Pupils may need to be reminded that their work does not have to look like a photograph: they have the freedom to take liberties with images – to exaggerate them, simplify them, distort them or even leave them out altogether.

Pupils working out of doors are faced with a barrage of potential images. Even indoors, it is easy to be distracted by surroundings (it may be helpful to place a screen, blank wall or large sheet of paper behind objects, to isolate them and enable pupils to focus on them). Pupils should be encouraged *not* to attempt to show everything: rather, to add detail to selected areas which will focus attention, and leave the rest impressionistic. Pupils may find a viewfinder useful: two L-shaped pieces of card that can be adjusted to create a makeshift frame through which to consider a desired composition. This may be mounted so that it projects above or to the side of the easel at which the pupil is working. Alternatively, using fingers and thumbs to create a makeshift oblong may suffice. Pupils will need to be taught how to return the viewfinder to the same position each time – this may be challenging for many pupils with learning difficulties. They may find it easier to use an old wooden picture frame placed at a suitable distance from where they are working, literally to 'frame' a view. Alternatively, considering the view as framed by a classroom or minibus window (see figure 6.7 p.61).

When working directly from observation to create *naturalistic* interpretations, pupils should be encouraged *not* to get 'bogged down' by concentrating on getting certain areas 'right', but rather to build up the whole image at the same time, and to note salient details. Conditions may easily change – 'models' move (be they people posing or animals on the loose!), and climatic conditions may quickly alter. Using a ruler may help with certain aspects – buildings for example, may have strong vertical and horizontal lines – but 'accuracy' should not overtake pupils' personal impressions. Teachers should beware their pupils becoming over-dependent on using a ruler – and on erasers, for that matter.

Scaling up the work may liberate pupils: working big and bold with a medium such as charcoal on a vertical surface and using large whole-arm movements from the shoulder. Pupils may make a quick outline sketch to familiarise themselves with proportions, and how representations will fit onto the 'support' (paper, canvas, etc). By screwing up their eyes, they may be able to see images out of focus, which will emphasise light and dark tones. Remember, erasers may be used also as a 'drawing' material – wiping areas that have been shaded to lighten them or to add highlights.

Alternatively, pupils may experiment with a range of art elements to make an abstract work, perhaps a freer interpretation of a chosen theme (see figure 5.6 p.39). These elements may appeal for their own sake (colour, shape, pattern, etc). This may be especially liberating for those pupils for whom the demands of subtle use of line and tone in more naturalistic representational work are technically challenging. For example: changing the colours, editing out various images, using certain textures to make patterns, apparently flattening images through attention to their outline shape rather than their three-dimensional form, adjusting the spatial arrangement of images.

Depicting images from different vantage points may give interest and intrigue to a work. Pupils may be encouraged to look at a subject they may wish to depict from all angles, before deciding on a particular viewpoint. Unexpected and surprising viewpoints can create an impact on the viewer: the artist's decision what *not* to show, or to partially conceal. The perception of pupils with learning difficulties may be challenged, by considering works by different artists who have explored an unusual perspective; for example, Burnham's 'Battle over Malta, 1942', depicted as if viewed from the cockpit of a fighter plane.

Using photographs

Pupils may find working from photographs easier than synthesising impressions directly 'in the field' – at least the subject matter remains static, and an image can be recreated at the pupils' own pace. As far as possible, pupils should be encouraged to use a sketchbook 'in the field', as a basis for recording their responses to experiences and personal reactions to salient aspects, and to prompt creative use of memory. However, pupils with learning difficulties may struggle with recall, depending on their memory span. Backing up field sketches with a photograph may facilitate recall of a scene, and give pupils an opportunity to supplement their field notes with additional information they may need. Photographs should be considered as a supplementary resource for art-making, in addition to, but not instead of, pupils' direct observations, memory and imagination.

However, there are significant *disadvantages* in using photographs to support art-making:

- There may be a danger that pupils may become over-reliant on the photograph, and be tempted slavishly to try to recreate every detail.

- Another disadvantage with photographs is that an editing process has already been carried out to a certain extent: what happens to be included or excluded from the frame.
- 'Snaps', by definition, are often hastily taken, without consideration for matters relating to composition and focal points of interest.
- Exact colours are unlikely to reproduce in a photograph.
- Photographs of images taken by other people, without first-hand observation by pupils 'in the field', may prevent pupils from grasping the scale and proportions and textural qualities of the subject matter.
- Photographs may preclude pupils from making their own personal interpretation of their subject, possibly preventing them from transforming their impressions, memory and imagination in the art-making process.

Pupils should be encouraged to use photographs *creatively:*
- Pupils may consider editing out features in photographs, focusing on certain aspects only, and leaving the rest impressionistic.
- By taking several photographs and shifting slightly each time, it is possible to build up a panoramic view from several photographs joined together, which may form the basis for a larger, sweeping landscape.
- Black and white photographs may help pupils to understand tones of images in their environment. This may be further exaggerated by taking photocopies (see *Art for All – The Practice*, figures 6.4 and 6.5).
- Details of images may be magnified using photography, and distant images brought into view by using telescopic lenses, thus offering pupils insights that they otherwise would not experience. This enhanced awareness may resource pupils' experimentation with the art elements, to record their responses.
- Photographs may be a useful prompt for reconstructing a still-life set-up that has to be disassembled between sessions.

CHAPTER 6

Shape, Form and Space

Shape, Form and Space in Art-Making

The development of shape, form and space in children's art-making is closely associated and embraces two aspects. Firstly, pupils' development in using these elements in the actual creation of images and artefacts themselves (two- and three-dimensional). Secondly, how images are expressed in relation to one another or their surroundings – in the overall composition of a piece of work. Pupils should be offered opportunities to reflect their growing understanding and knowledge of shape, form and space, in both two- and three-dimensional art-making experiences. Formal teaching about composition – for example, perspective or focal points – will be inappropriate for many pupils with learning difficulties. Nevertheless, if teachers have a grasp of some of the principles involved, they may then be able to construct a method to help their pupils *understand* how a particular impression may be achieved.

Direct experience of the shape and *form* of objects and artefacts will inform and underpin pupils' interpretations of the natural and made environment: considering their structure, feel, character and design. Some pupils with learning difficulties may find the solidity and manageability of made artefacts easier than certain delicate natural objects, when considering properties of shape and form. Insight gained from direct experiences may be transferred to reproducing images at all levels of ability: whether recreating what is *known* from memory in the case of the work of developmentally young children or, later, what is *seen* from direct observational studies.

Pupils need to learn to recognise and use *shape* as part of their visual language. Objects and artefacts in the natural and made environment are comprised of shapes of all kinds: regular, irregular, simple and complex. Shapes may be explored for their own sake, in creating abstract arrangements in a range of materials and media – random or ordered, overlapping or tessellating. Malleable materials (dough, clay, plasticene) will offer possibilities for pupils to create their own shapes.

Pupils may discover how shapes resonate with one another – the effect of angular or curved shapes. Artists such as Kandinsky, Malevich, Mondrian, Miro, Robert and Sonia Delaunay, and German Expressionists such as Marc and Macke, and Klee, were particularly intrigued by arrangements of shapes and their effect on the viewer (see figure 6.1 p.66). Their techniques are very accessible to pupils of all ages and abilities, and may be readily harnessed in pupils' art-making in a range of two- and three-dimensional media, both in abstract work and for suggesting representational imagery. For example, consideration of the work in figure 6.1 may prompt pupils' own art-making using rectangles in primary colours, or using a range of media for the edges of shapes (e.g. art straws, threads, string, ribbons, etc).

Developing Understanding of Shape, Form and Space

Knowledge and attention to details of images develops in parallel with pupils' growing awareness of the relative position of images to one another. Pupils' imagery (abstract and/or representational) may gradually become more ordered and integrated within a composition, with greater selectivity over use of *space*. This development cannot be forced: the way through is to encourage pupils' awareness of objects in juxtaposition rather than in isolation, but not to insist on a representation beyond their stage of development. Equally, attention to the placement of images in abstract work may become similarly ordered and considered. The spaces the artist leaves are just as important as the marks or images themselves, just as periods of silence in music are important for establishing rhythm.

1 Early tactile *experience of the properties of a range of materials* (rigid and malleable) will lay the foundations for pupils' subsequent development of their understanding and use of the elements of shape, form and space in art-making. For example: squeezing, flattening and poking at clay; manipulating 'found' sources and combining them to make an abstract three-dimensional construction; 'feely' activities (e.g. identifying objects in a bag by touch) and early experiences of sorting and categorising items for their shape (solid, round, flat or straight-sided), which may also be used as a resource for art-making. Early discovery of basic cause-effect ('I can make that mark there') will be random and haphazard, with *marks gradually placed with increasing selectivity* over the 'support' (see figure 4.1 p.37).

2 Pupils' early mark-making develops from lines of different kinds, to *defining shapes by enclosing lines, and making complex diagrammatic* forms by combining lines and marks (see figure 5.1). These may or may not be symbolic. For example, a pupil may combine and reform lumps of clay, which subsequently suggest a creature. Pupils may select collage pieces of different shapes and sizes to select within a prescribed area, although placement of items may be somewhat irregular, with *limited regard for the suitability of size match to space available.*

3 Pupils may progress to a greater *awareness and control of the size and shape of features in their art-making.* Pupils may select and combine shapes to make images (representational and/or abstract), with an awareness of their spatial placement; for example, they may select collage items of a particular size to fit available spaces. Representational images may appear to float (see figure 2.1), with sizes and details reflecting their importance and significance to the child, rather than their actual proportions.

4 Gradually *images may become more ordered within a composition;* for example, pupils may experiment in collage work with abstract arrangements of items to produce a regular pattern, or make a slab picture from moulding rolls of clay.

Representational images may be lined up along a base-line – there may even be multi-base-lines; for example, simplifed representation of ground and sky at top and bottom of the page, with features depicted in a line, but not overlapping (see figure 6.2 p.40). Pupils' work may indicate greater awareness of real-life size relationships, although they may find it difficult to reproduce representations of objects on the same scale. It may be that they are intrigued by one object's patterning or colour, yet produce an outline of another object. Pupils' awareness of the relative size or placement of images may be fostered through themes where these are inherently emphasised; for example, 'playing football', 'my family', etc.

5 Pupils may progress to *integrating images in a plane within a composition* (see figure 5.2 p.40); for example, they may create a design from geometric shapes for a T-shirt that takes account of the whole surface area. Pupils' representational work may indicate an integrated horizon, with the skyline brought down to the ground. This awareness may be encouraged through themes that prompt attention to filling in a 'plane', with objects in relation to one another; e.g. 'the table set for dinner'. Pupils may be taught about 'negative shapes' (the spaces between images) as well as 'positive shapes' (the images themselves), with awareness and attention to their relative sizes, whether in representational or abstract work. Pupils may work from direct observation, to make interpretations of groups of objects of a similar size; for example, in a still-life set-up – or from part of the set-up, if not the whole group.

6 Pupils may become preoccupied with *portraying volume of images, and creating a sense of depth to their work*. For example, they may sculpt a free-standing figure by carving into a lump of clay, with attention to detail and proportion (see figure 6.3). They may overlap shapes and images of different sizes and colours in two-dimensional work, to create a sense of perspective. For example, they may arrange overlapping shapes in different colours along diagonal axes in the style of Malevich, to create a sense of movement according to whether they appear to 'advance' or 'recede' (see chapter 4). In naturalistic work, they may harness certain techniques used by other artists, concerning composition and perspective.

Using Shape, Form and Space

This section makes certain points relating to composition in two-dimensional art (based largely on Smith, 1994, amongst others). Notions of 'composition' carry connotations of formal, technical training, which easily has a 'de-skilling' effect on many non-specialist teachers of art. However, basic pointers and principles may assist teachers in supporting certain pupils at their art-making, and helping them to appreciate how other artists have used and suggested shape, form and space in their work. Understanding certain principles governing composition may also be useful in designing friezes of children's work, and for creating effects within the classroom environment. This may be particularly pertinent for attracting the attention of certain pupils with learning difficulties, to notice areas of interest in their surroundings.

The 'format'

A difficulty for teachers creating a frieze is that the 'format' is usually already imposed – dictated by the shape of the pinboard. The same is true for pupils, if they are not encouraged to *question* the format of the piece of paper presented to them – that is,

Figure 6.3 *'Woman' (clay sculpture, by pupil with severe learning difficulties). This pupil has carved into the clay to create the three-dimensional form, with detailed attention to sex characteristics, posture and expression of the figure.*

the shape and orientation of the 'support' (paper, canvas, board, etc). Teachers tend to present pupils automatically with a standard oblong format. Pupils need to learn to make informed decisions about which format will best suit their intentions. If pupils are not encouraged to think ahead, they may end up inadvertently compromising their intentions, with images squashed or distorted to fit the space available, rather than deliberately intended (see figure 6.4).

If pupils are making a portrait, it may be more appropriate for them to work on a vertical oblong format, to follow the form of the human body. If they are wanting to depict a sweeping landscape, it may be more appropriate to work on a horizontal oblong format. Vertical formats will tend to draw the viewer's eye upwards, whereas horizontal formats will encourage the viewer's gaze to flow across the support. If an illusion of space surrounding an image is significant (for example, figures or boats on the move), then working on a horizontal format may give that impression. If the sky or a particular feature in the distance is the focus of attention, then it may be more appropriate to work on a vertical oblong format, rather than show a broad horizon.

If pupils have a clear idea of particular images they wish to represent, it may be that logically, their shapes will fit into a particular format; pupils may be encouraged to envisage their proportions, and judge the viability of a vertical or horizontal oblong format accordingly. Alternatively, pupils may consider *whereabouts* they wish the viewer's attention to be drawn – whether the area of main interest will be near the top or near the bottom; in the case of the former, the horizontal format may be preferable, and if the latter, the vertical format may be favoured. Many pupils with learning difficulties may find it challenging, however, to envisage an image they may wish to achieve, and its potential impact on the viewer.

Pupils may also consider the *mood* they may wish to convey – this abstract notion will be challenging for many pupils with learning difficulties, but could be important. They may wish to achieve a 'cosy' feeling of intimacy or convergence (drawing the viewer's attention inwards); alternatively, a sense of expansiveness or

Figure 6.4: *'Govind' (drawing in blue felt pen by junior pupil with severe learning difficulties). This boy has distorted the torso and legs of the figure, to fit the space available. If he had been encouraged to think through his work, and opted for a vertical format, he may have had more scope for creating a more conventionally proportioned figure.*

divergence (drawing the viewer's attention outwards). They may then decide which format will be most suitable – vertical or horizontal, respectively.

Teachers may choose to challenge pupils' exploration of space, by deliberately presenting them with different shaped formats – for example, a square, circle or an exaggerated oblong. Many twentieth-century artists deliberately opt to challenge the rectangular format – e.g. Mondrian's rhomboid canvases. Historically, rectangular formats only really became popular when pictures started to be exhibited alongside each other, as they fitted more neatly into hanging space. Previously, artists were used to adapting images within all kinds of regular and irregular spaces – for example, witness the frescoes and ceiling paintings of Michelangelo.

Of all shapes other than the rectangle, traditionally the circular format was the most common. The *circle* presents different challenges with regard to composition, as the viewer's eye is led round and round, as opposed to off and out as with rectangular formats; artists tend to use 'stabilising' devices, such as strong vertical and horizontal lines. An *oval* format also invites the viewer's eye to move round and round, but has something of the characteristics of vertical or horizontal rectangular formats. A *square* format will yield a stable, compact impression, and draw the viewer's attention to the centre; this is exemplified in Monet's classic painting of the bridge over the lily pond in his garden at Giverny.

Focal points

Artists manipulate aspects of composition, to draw the viewer's attention to strategic focal points, with 'restful' areas in between. There may be one main area of interest, or more than one focal point; these have to be reconciled, so that images do not 'shout' at each other. Artists may also employ a range of other devices to attract the viewer's attention.

Priority features – one main area of interest:

- Placing an image directly in the *centre* of a composition will necessarily attract attention, as this tends to be where the viewer's gaze focuses first. It can easily become over-dominant, however, or over-emphasise symmetry and inadvertently have the effect of apparently cutting a composition in half; for this reason, many artists actually tend to place a focal point off-centre.
- Placing an image *off-centre* will draw the viewer's attention, but also encourage the viewer's eye to rove over the surrounding context of the image. Artists commonly use the 'rule of thirds' to place a focal point off-centre, whereby the format (whether vertical or horizontal) is divided into *vertical thirds* (see figure 6.5), and an image (e.g. a prominent feature or figure) is placed strategically along one of the imaginary dividing lines. This is particularly significant for creating the impression of an image 'on the move': it either needs space to move into, or else a suggestion that it has just left a space, by partially 'cropping' the image, as if leaving the frame.
- In a landscape, placing the horizon straight across the middle will have the same effect as above, and cause the composition to appear chopped in half. The artist may consider whether the sky or the foreground is the main interest. If the former, the sky may be emphasised by placing the horizon lower; if the latter, then the horizon may be placed higher. A format can also be divided into *horizontal thirds* (see figure 6.5), whereby points of interest (such as the horizon in this example) are placed a third of the way from the top or bottom, along the imaginary dividing lines. The same principle may apply to other important images, whether figures should be placed to the top or bottom of the composition. If they are placed in the top third, this will accentuate foreground details and give an impression of space and remoteness.
- The Ancient Greeks and Romans originally devised a precise formula for creating perfect harmony in a composition, known as the *Golden Section*, which approximates to dividing a rectangular format into two unequal sections along both axes, to end up with an off-centre cross. It is not suggested that the placing of a key feature should be so precisely worked out! However, positioning an important image either in a particular section, or directly along the imaginary Golden Section lines, may have the effect of giving a sense of proportion and balance.

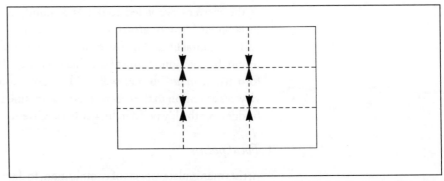

Figure 6.5: *Devices for composition: the 'rule of thirds' and the 'four key points', created at the intersection of imaginary lines.*

Multiple points of interest:

- If a composition is divided into imaginary vertical and horizontal thirds, where they cross will yield *four key points* (see figure 6.5 p.58) – these may serve as focal points for important images to be placed, provided they do not compete with one another for the viewer's attention.
- Focal points may be *graded,* so that one is obviously more important than the others, through selective use of scale, tone and colour – for example, an important image prominently in the foreground, but with a second image smaller in the background, but depicted in white or red to draw the eye.
- Two focal points may be placed at a distance apart – however, this may have a ping-pong effect if they are too far apart, as the viewer's eye will bounce between the two. This may be avoided by placing them diagonally on two of the four key points.
- If there are multiple focal points, the viewer's eye needs to travel evenly over the composition. Areas of interest may be balanced over the format; for example, a group portrait or landscape scene, or diagonally on the four key points.
- Scattering focal points randomly over the composition will have the effect of emphasising distribution of images, and decorative or patterning aspects, as these will 'anchor' the viewer's eye. Brueghel, Avercamp and Lowry employed this technique in their works.

Attention-drawing devices:

- Certain sinewy features encourage the eye to travel along them; e.g. fences, paths, hedges, streams, etc. Also, the horizon itself, which may be a long gentle curve or else broken and undulating.
- Important images may be 'framed'; e.g. by a natural arch or span in a landscape, or else by a doorway or window for interiors.
- A 'closed' composition will 'block' the viewer's eye and prevent it from wandering out of frame – this may be achieved by strategically 'framing' an image; e.g. looking through a 'window' of vegetation at a significant feature.
- 'Open' compositions will allow the eye to travel expansively; for example, an unbroken horizon towards the top third of a landscape may draw the eye away from features in the foreground. In order to draw the viewer's eye back into the composition, features in the foreground or middleground may be depicted large, and project and break the horizon (see figure 6.6 p.11).
- Strategic use of colour will be effective in drawing attention: a 'hot' colour amongst 'cold' colours, or a bright tone against a muted background (see figure 6.6).
- Converging 'pathways' will lead the eye to a point of interest.
- Diagonals, sweeping circles or swirling lines will create a sense of vigour, and will cause the viewer's eye to flow over the composition.
- Linking important images strategically along 'pathways' that form an imaginary triangle will create a sense of stability along the 'base', with a 'peak' of interest.
- Use of strong vertical and horizontal lines will keep the eye moving as if along a grid, but without being drawn into the picture; this will tend to emphasise patterning details on surfaces.

Perspective

Significantly, developmentally young children will automatically mix perspectives and draw images in a way that will convey most information – cars from side view, but people and buildings face-on. Artistic traditions and cultures have varied considerably in how images have been depicted in relation to each other. Pupils may consider the art of Ancient Egypt, with the torso of figures portrayed apparently facing fully to the front, yet heads and limbs in profile. Aboriginal art reflects a birds-eye view, with images depicted as if observed from above, instead of from the side as in western art traditions.

The sense of 'realism' in two-dimensional naturalistic works in contemporary western culture stems from the Italian Renaissance in the fourteenth century, whereby images were represented as seen from a single, fixed viewpoint – known as *single-point perspective*. Twentieth-century art has deliberately challenged this, as epitomised in the work of the Cubist artists, who showed several planes of an image at the same time. Playing down tonal variations will have the effect of flattening the form of images, and emphasising colour and shape at the expense of spatial aspects – a device which has been used considerably in twentieth-century art. Picasso once commented that it had taken him a lifetime to learn to draw like a child!

Pupils may consider how different artists have created a sense of depth and distance to their work, and maybe harness techniques in their own art-making (see figure 6.7 p.65). Certain techniques may give an illusion of depth to a composition:

- The farther away an object is meant to be, the higher it may be placed in the picture; the 'Naive' artists used this technique.
- The more distant the object, the smaller it may be compared to images close-to depicted large; Hokusai's work showed the influence of this technique, gleaned from western artistic tradition.
- The position of an object in relation to the picture frame may give an impression of distance: 'cropped' images, apparently half out of frame, will seem close to, whereas a whole image depicted centrally will appear more distant from the 'window' of the picture frame.
- Overlapping images will give an illusion of depth, such that those more distant are partially concealed, even though in actuality they may be drawn as shapes next to each other.
- The closer an object, the more detail of texturing will be apparent – this will emphasise the foreground, compared to background images which may be depicted untextured.
- Using 'hot' colours in the foreground will make images 'advance', and using 'cooler' colours for the middleground and background features will make images 'recede'.
- Exploiting *aerial* or *atmospheric perspective,* will make images appear less bright the more distant they are (e.g. a bright red telephone box will appear browner); distant images will appear less distinct, with outlines and details blurred, and less contrast between areas of light and dark.
- Aerial perspective applies to landscapes *and* skyscapes – depicting a tonal range that lightens towards the horizon, with darker tones at the top of the picture for the sky, and at the bottom for the land, will give a sense of the sky and land receding, with lighter tones close together at the junction of the horizon.
- Exploring a tonal range will give an apparent sense of depth – images may be exactly the same size, but those shaded darker will seem nearer than those shaded more lightly.
- Parallel lines (such as the top and bottom of a building, or the edges of a path or road) apparently narrowing and converging to a point (known as the *vanishing point*) in the distance will give a sense of depth.
- Circular images will become ellipses when they are perceived from a distance.

CHAPTER 7

Understanding and Appreciating Art

Reading Images

In introducing pupils to their artistic heritage, the aim is *not* to adopt a 'history of art' approach of potted biographies of different artists. Van Gogh may have cut off his ear, and Toulouse-Lautrec happened to be short; however, their treatment of subject matter and the techniques they used are of far greater significance to the teaching of art. Pupils need to learn to 'read images' for their explicit and implicit meanings: to be empowered to make sense of their world, by developing an understanding of an artist's intentions. Considering the work of other artists will offer pupils insight into different cultures and traditions, and enjoyment of their artistic heritage, to inspire and inform their own art-making.

Pupils need to learn to discriminate, select and judge works of art for themselves. Teachers need to be very honest and aware of their own personal preferences, in order not to let that affect pupils' reactions and responses: for example, pupils may quickly pick up if their teacher dismisses an abstract painting by Picasso in favour of a more naturalistic one by Constable. Even a phrase like 'look at the nice bright colours' may be an instant give-away, and inadvertently deter pupils subsequently from respecting (for example) a sketch in black chalk by Van Gogh.

It is important that pupils are presented with a range of both two- and three-dimensional works from different cultures and historical times, by male and female artists, in order to broaden their horizons and awareness. Even if they do not have a precise grasp of the geographical origin of a work, or an established concept of time to understand exactly how long ago it was created, pupils with learning difficulties may still benefit from being exposed to a range of art styles and traditions. Works should be presented in a way that will enable pupils to engage with them and perceive their relevance and significance in terms of their own experience.

The point of contact for the pupils with a particular work may be the subject matter or content, the technique used or perhaps the particular use and emphasis on certain visual elements. Pupils should be helped to understand something of the context in which the works were created. Pupils might consider, for example, why particular materials were used, depending on their availability. What kind of person was the artist, if known (rich? poor? royal? religious?). Was the work created for a particular reason, purpose or occasion?

In reading images, pupils need to learn to recognise how an artist has used the *visual elements* described in chapters 3, 4, 5 and 6: pattern and texture, colour, line and tone, and shape, form and space. Maybe certain visual elements have been emphasised and others played down; for example, the sombre colours of Van Gogh's early work of Dutch peasants, compared to his later vibrant landscapes of southern France, and how that reflected his personal circumstances and the place in which he painted.

Pupils may be made aware of the *historical context* influencing certain works; for example, the availability of manufactured pigments provided a more extensive range of colour tones in paints, such that late nineteenth- and twentieth-century paintings are often (but not exclusively) much more vibrant than earlier works. The introduction of fresh oil paint in tubes freed artists to be able to work in this medium out of doors – in Turner's later work, it is possible to identify where he has squeezed paint directly onto the canvas. The Impressionist painters were similarly liberated, and many aimed to complete a work in a day, painting fast and spontaneously before the light and weather conditions changed.

A distinction may be made between works of art created *before* and *after* the advent of *photography*. Prior to the camera, artists commissioned to produce a 'likeness', or naturalistic representation of a person or place, were reliant on accurate observation and 'photographic memory' of their subjects, noting details meticulously in sketchbooks. Some artists harnessed techniques in painting and drawing: for example, images partially out of frame (as in the work of Degas), background images out of focus (as in the work of Lord Leighton). Many artists subsequently rejected photography, liberated from faithful or naturalistic reproductions, because the camera could perform that function. Instead, they opted to work on a more emotional level, reflecting their reactions and feelings about their subject matter, or else indulging in exploration of the art media for its own sake, in more abstract work. For example, the emancipation of colour in the work of Van Gogh and Fauvist artists such as Vlaminck, Derain and Matisse.

Other artists have embraced photography, both as a tool to resource their art-making in other media, and also as an art form in its own right. Hockney developed a technique which he called 'photocollage', where several photographs are taken from the same viewpoint and assembled to give panoramic view. Influenced by the work of the Cubist artists, Hockney made fragmented photocollages with multi-perspectives (the same image photographed from different angles), and different planes of the same image, to capture several moments and include a sense of narrative. For example, 'The Scrabble Game' shows several views of each player around the board, which conveys a sense of 'story' about the game.

Pupils may be made aware of possible *bias* in works of art. Even though it may look naturalistic, a work may still be susceptible to deliberate distortion by the artist, particularly if working to commission. Bearing in mind 'customer satisfaction', would portrait artists *always* have produced a faithful, accurate 'likeness' of their subject? Remember the trouble Holbein had when he painted an over-flattering portrait of Anne of Cleves to endear her to King Henry VIII! How accurately could a seventeenth-century artist honestly have portrayed the children of wealthy families – how long would they realistically have posed for the artist without fidgeting? Isn't it more likely that artists would have curried favour from their wealthy benefactors by painting their offspring a little too angelically?

Pupils may consider the *political context* of certain works of art – for example, official war artists were required to glorify war as opposed to expressing any protest; and what about propaganda posters – what was the artist *really* saying? Can pupils sort a collection of reproductions of images of war by different artists, according to those who thought war was a good thing or a bad thing? They may make their own interpretation of the theme of war: glorifying it or expressing their dislike (see figure 5.6 p.39).

Pupils may consider the *social context* of a work – for example, why are there relatively few portraits from earlier centuries of poorer strata of society? Pupils may glean historical information from works of art. Some will show specific moments in history, and portraits of significant figures; others will reveal information of the time – clothing, buildings, lifestyles, technology, etc. Pupils may be encouraged to look at background details and objects and artefacts represented in a work – do they provide additional clues about the subject matter or perhaps what the artist is trying to tell us? The artist may have deliberately included features that are symbolic: e.g. a family portrait where the members are engaged in music-making, to imply a sense of 'harmony' and family unity; or a portrait where the figure is surrounded by snakes, skulls and other images associated with 'death', to imply that the person is deceased. Pupils could compare portraits of the Royal Family over time – why are present members depicted more informally than their relatives from previous generations? Pupils might like to consider their *own* portrait: what clothes they would like to wear, what things they would like to have with them, and also where would they like to be shown? Indoors? Outdoors? In a favourite room?

Pupils may compare different artists' treatment of similar themes, and express and justify their ideas, opinions and feelings. The teacher's skill in questioning will be crucial, in enabling pupils to share their reactions: maybe employing a hierarchy of questioning (see chapter 2), starting with an open question, and gradually narrowing the parameters towards more closed questions. Pupils' ability to relate to the work of other artists will reflect their own stage of development in art-making, and the way they perceive and organise information.

Developing Understanding of Art

Pupils' knowledge and understanding of artistic methods has to be grounded in their own direct experience of different forms of art making, using a range of tools and materials. From this basis, they may be able to recognise other examples of work using the same methods in their surroundings – starting in the immediate school environment, and gradually making connections further afield, with examples of work in the community. Their appreciation of other artists' approaches will parallel their own growth in art-making, and the way the different visual elements may be combined and emphasised in different art forms (see figures 7.1, 7.2 and 7.3 p.66 and 67).

The point of contact with a work should be appropriate for pupils to absorb and embrace ideas and approaches in their own work. Pupils may grasp something of a particular artist's philosophy, provided that it is presented in a way that is relevant to their own experience. For example, about Matisse's portrait of Derain (see figure 7.1): 'he wanted to use colours that showed he liked this person... What are your favourite colours? What colours make you feel happy? What colours make you feel sad?', etc.

1 Pupils may learn to *associate different tools and materials with a particular art practice*. For example, they may sign 'modelling', 'drawing', 'painting' when presented with clay, crayons/felt pens, or brush and paint respectively. Pupils may distinguish different art forms within the school and immediate locality. For example, they may identify a painting, drawing, print, collage or sculpture. This may be fostered by presenting works to pupils, then immediately following this up with art-making that harnesses similar use of the art elements (colour, shape, etc) in the same medium (see figure 7.4 p.68).

2 Pupils may *grasp that works of art may express an aspect of experience*. They may recognise readily identifiable images or forms in works: picking out familiar objects, geometric shapes, etc, and be challenged to identify features in increasingly abstract work. Pupils may include similar themes in their own art-making.

3 Pupils may *recognise how a work was created, by commenting on distinctive features and particular use of visual and tactile elements*. For example, the swirling lines and facial distortion in Munch's 'The Scream'. Comments may refer to obvious aspects: 'he's used lots of yellow paint'; 'it's not coloured in'; 'there's lots of squares and oblongs', etc. Pupils may emulate appealing or intriguing features in their own art-making (see figure 7.2).

4 Pupils may *identify in the school and in the locality the materials and methods used to create a particular work*. For example, recognising a sculpture in the park that has been carved from wood with chisels. Their own art-making may reflect a growing ability to recreate particular effects, using a range of tools, materials and techniques in the work of other artists.

5 Pupils may *compare the way different artists have treated similar themes, and consider their respective use of the art elements more systematically* with attention to detail (see figure 7.3). For example, they may compare the use of colour in landscapes by Derain and Matisse with those by Constable and Gainsborough. Their own interpretations of subject matter may reveal a preferred artistic style.

6 Pupils may *grasp the social, historical and cultural context of a work*. For example, they may identify examples of 'pop art' (works by Lichenstein and Warhol), and associate them with modern times, specifically the influence of mass visual media. Pupils may use an artist's approach as a starting point, to consolidate their own expression in their preferred media, perhaps deviating considerably from an original stimulus (see *Art for All – The Practice,* figure 5.3).

Figure 6.7: *'Coltishall Broad' (drawing in coloursticks by senior pupil with moderate learning difficulties). This girl has experimented with several techniques to create a sense of perspective to her sketch: greater texture given to the foreground, and images in the distance depicted smaller, with a narrower tonal range.*

Figure 7.1: 'Portrait of Andre Derain' (1905) by Henri Matisse (Tate Gallery, London). © Succession H. Matisse/DACS 1996

Figure 6.1: 'Composition with Grey, Red, Yellow and Blue (1920-6)' by Piet Mondrian (Tate Gallery, London)

66

Figure 7.3 Interpretation of Matisse's 'Portrait of Andre Derain' (painting in cromar paints by an eight year old pupil in mainstream). This boy (at a more advanced stage in his art-making than the artist in Figure 7.2) was intrigued by Matisse's Fauvist style. He imitated Matisse's approach: his brush work, his use of complementary colours and tones of colour, and built up his picture in the same way as the artist, sketching in rough outlines in paint, painting the background, and then working the head by overlaying colours.

Figure 7.2 Interpretation of Matisse's 'Portrait of Andre Derain' (oil pastel drawing, by a junior pupil with severe learning difficulties). This boy usually only obsessively drew cars, but quite spontaneously was attracted by a reproduction on the art room wall (figure 7.1), particularly Derain's red beret; his choice of colours has broadly reflected those of the artist, Matisse.

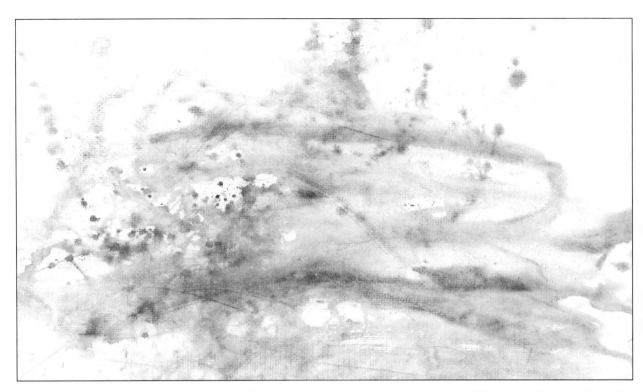

Figure 7.4: *Wet on wet painting by pupil with profound and multiple learning difficulties. This pupil applied water in broad washes, then brushed and spattered dilute powder colour. This experience followed immediately from looking at slides of Turner's sunsets, accompanied by a tape of Beethoven's 'Pastoral Symphony'. Colours have been restricted to prompt a resonance between the slides and the pupil's own work.*

Figure 7.5: *'Flowers' (painting by senior pupil with severe learning difficulties). This girl has imitated Monet's Impressionist style, to show her own garden.*

Developing Responses to Art

Pupils of all ages and abilities should be enabled to respond to works of art, craft and design, including their own and others' work. This may entail imaginative presentation by the teacher, in order for certain pupils to notice and engage with them (see figure 7.4 p.68). Pupils need to be enabled to evaluate art in a way that is appropriate and relevant to their ability and experience. For example, developmentally young pupils should not be expected to comment on an artist's use of perspective, as this will be alien to their conceptual grasp.

1 Pupils may *react positively or negatively to works of art.* For example, flinching at the rough texture of a sculpture carved from wood, but smiling at the smooth texture of a sculpture cast in bronze. Magnifying and projecting slides of two-dimensional works onto a wall in a darkened room may draw pupils' attention and evoke a response. A multi-sensory approach to presenting works may be appropriate: sound tapes of noises featuring in various works, feeling different tactile surfaces in collages, sculptures, impasto paintings, etc. It may be possible to take advantage of sensory exhibitions and handling sessions at museums and galleries.

2 Pupils may respond to the ideas, methods or approaches used in different artistic styles and traditions, by *commenting on distinctive aspects.* In the same way that pupils will prioritise certain images in their own art-making, to reflect important or significant aspects from their experience, so they may draw on their life-experience to make connections with images in the works of other artists. This may entail 'stating the obvious' with regard to commenting on the content or subject matter of a piece. For example, discussing the activities of characters in works by Lowry or Brueghel; discussing how Modigliani exaggerated the length of his subject's faces.

3 As pupils become more preoccupied with detail in their own work, so they may be able to *attend to how an artist suggests (for example) pattern and texture.* For example, commenting on embellishment and decoration on costume in portraits by Reynolds; noting how Picasso achieves an impression of wood by using a herring-bone pattern, etc.

4 As their experience of art-making broadens, they may *comment more systematically on how a work was created,* as well as describing it in simple terms and offering their thoughts and feelings.

5 Once pupils are becoming aware of creating a sense of depth and/or volume to images in their own work, they may *consider how other artists have achieved an impression of three-dimensionality.* For example, noting how Constable created a sense of perspective in his landscapes, with features in the distance portrayed small.

6 Pupils may be encouraged to *use appropriate art, craft and design vocabulary and to draw on their knowledge* to substantiate their ideas and opinions about a work and the context in which it was created.

Pupils will need access to examples of work from a wide range of different art styles and traditions. This requires teachers to collate a resource bank of reproductions. The better the quality of the reproduction, the more pupils will gain appreciation of artists' use of the visual elements, such as colour and texture (e.g. how thickly paint has been applied, the direction of brush strokes, etc). Class discussion should be based around a large reproduction – pupils with learning difficulties may well have perceptual problems with anything smaller. It is worth asking around the staffroom, to see if anyone has a required reproduction that is of a suitable size. Some education authorities, clusters of schools, teachers' centres and local museums and galleries may operate an art loan scheme of framed reproductions and/or slides. Educational journals may also provide suitable resources – pull-out posters with suggestions for using them with pupils.

Pupils will also need smaller, more manageable reproductions from which to work on table tops. These should be laminated and mounted on card for protection from the rigours of practical art activity. Old calendars are often excellent sources – make sure friends, colleagues and pupils' parents save them after Christmas! Certain educational suppliers and museums and galleries now provide packs of appropriate reproductions for school use. Greetings cards and art postcards are also useful, although too small as a focus for discussion with a class group. However, they may be useful for individual pupils working alone, with a magnifying class for closer examination. Postcards tend to offer limited possiblities, however, as certain details may be imprecise on such a small scale.

All reproductions have their limitations. There can be no substitute for visits to galleries and seeing artists at work. If pupils are only ever presented with small prints or postcards, they may never appreciate the different scales and sizes of works of art; for example, Matisse's 'The Snail' (see figure 2.2 p.10) would occupy a whole wall! It is an interesting exercise for pupils to have reproductions ahead of a visit to a gallery, and then compare them with the originals. Certain qualities are lost in reproductions; for example, true shades and tints of colours, the texture of a painting, etc. Even more can be lost in postcard-sized two-dimensional reproduction of a three-dimensional work; for example, what a sculpture is like from all directions, its tactile quality, size, weight, mass, smell, its location and the sense of awe it may inspire.

Recurrent themes in art include the following:

- people: portraits, relationships;
- environments: natural (landscapes, seascapes, skyscapes, etc) and made (cityscapes, interiors, etc);
- animals: domestic, wild;
- plants, trees, flowers, etc;
- objects: natural and made (still life);
- events: historical, personal, social;
- fantastic: myths and legends, stories, metamorphosis, dreams;
- abstract: form, meaning, emotions.

When presenting the work of artists to a class as a stimulus, it is possible to work through three stages:

Looking and responding

Opportunity for pupils to express their 'gut reaction' to a piece of work, and to comment on it freely. Pose open-ended questions: 'Do you like it? Why? Why not?'... Pupils are perfectly justified in *not* liking a work of art, but they should be encouraged to substantiate their opinion. Do not necessarily tell pupils the title of the work straightaway – what would *they* call it? Does it remind them of anything? *Then* tell them the artist's title.

The pupils might also consider the effect of different *frames* on a two-dimensional work, and the location of a three-dimensional sculpture. There have been distinct fashions in framing two-dimensional works. In the nineteeth century, works could be rejected by the Paris Salon if they were not in a traditional gilt frame. Many artists customise their own frames; certain types of frames were even named after particular artists (e.g. the Whistler frame, the Seurat frame, etc). Van Gogh considered that a work was not complete until it had a frame, and made his own flat pine mouldings which he overpainted. A frame may be chosen to:

- distinguish the work from its surroundings;
- link the work with its surroundings, as an extension of the painting or its context;
- complement or contradict the work, and draw attention to itself.

Developing a response

More in-depth consideration of the work may have the effect of enhancing the pupils' appreciation of the work on closer examination. Through structuring the discussion, feed in further information and heighten the pupils' awareness of artists' intentions through their use of the art elements. Examples of questions and discussion points:

- *Content* What is it about? How can you tell? Does it tell a story? What do you think the artist is trying to tell us? What sort of noises would be associated with it? What sort of music would go with it?
- *Historical questions* What can we find out by looking at this? Does it show things as they are nowadays? Or is it in days gone by? What things are different from nowadays? Why was it done and for whom? (Bias? Artist working to commission? Political context?)
- *Social history* Fashions, buildings, landscape, rich/poor? Look at backgrounds as well as the main focal points for additional clues. What are their clothes like? Do you recognise any of the buildings? Do they look like clothes (or buildings) that we see nowadays? Where is this picture painted? Is it inside or outdoors? What kind of a place is it? Is that person rich or poor, old or young? How can you tell? What is s/he holding? How do they look – happy? sad? angry? Do you think they know (or like) each other? How can we tell?
- *Artistic questions* How the work was created, how certain effects were achieved, use of the art elements (line, colour, space, etc). Does it look real? Why/why not? How does it make you feel? Why? What kind of colours have been used? What if different colours were used? When in the artist's career was the work created? How is this significant? (e.g. Effect of limited colour pigments? Before the advent of photography? etc). How could the artist have

remembered exactly what something or somewhere looked like, if the final work was to be completed in the studio?

Consolidating a response

Offer pupils opportunities to follow up their observations in practical activity; apart from art-making, this could also entail music, drama, and/or creative writing. Examples of follow-up work:

Drama

- Create 'tableaux vivants' of the work, where pupils adopt the stance of characters in a painting or sculpture, which can then come to life and be 'frozen' again at any moment. What are the characters thinking? What are they saying to one another? Use 'think bubbles' and 'speech bubbles' cut from card – are they the same? Allow children observing to question characters, and then bring them to life in a short improvisation.
- Show what happened just before/just afterwards (in frozen tableaux or short improvisation).
- Teacher-in-role could talk directly to the pupils either as a character in a work, or even as the artist him/herself.
- Maybe focus on just a *part* of the work, or on just one aspect of it; e.g. What are two of the figures in the background saying to each other? Who are they? Develop into a pairs improvisation, or mime the conversation to emphasise use of body language.

  (NB Refer to *Drama For All* (Peter, 1994) and *Making Drama Special* (Peter, 1995) for strategies on using drama with pupils with learning difficulties).

Writing

- Write the story of the work of art – maybe told through the eyes of one of the characters portrayed, or even one of the objects. For example, of Van Gogh's chair: 'If this chair could speak, what would it tell you?'.
- Describe the work of art from memory.
- Write about 'what happened next' or 'what happened just beforehand'.

Art

- Mould characters or objects in a two-dimensional work in to a three-dimensional art form.
- Copy the style/certain techniques – maybe concentrate on just part of the work.
- Consider the effect of changing elements; e.g. 'what if....those sunflowers were blue'...). Use to stimulate pupils' own picture-making.
- Copy the same picture, but using different media, on a different scale, etc.
- Draw/paint the work of art from memory.
- Compare work on a similar theme by different artists.

Music

- Compose an evocative soundscape by layering voices imitating aspects in a picture (e.g. seaside, garden, countryside, built-up area): consider background, middleground and foreground sounds – those which are continuous and those which are intermittent.

- Compose the story of the work, using instruments to reflect a narrative – develop beyond the image, to include what happened immediately before and/or afterwards.
- Compose music to convey the mood of the work: scary? happy? sad? loud? quiet?
- Reflect visual elements in an abstract work through use of elements in music, giving structure to a composition by linking sound to symbol (*NB* this may need to be simplified, with certain motifs selected or a part of a picture isolated); e.g. patterning to suggest rhythm; colour to suggest harmony or discord and dynamics (loud or quiet); texture to suggest solo or ensemble playing or singing; line to suggest tempo (fast and energetic, or smooth and sustained); tone to suggest strong contrasts or gradations of contrast in the music; shapes and form to suggest kinds of sounds (angular: harsh, curving: gentle); use of space to suggest a structure for the music (e.g. a particular pathway through the work).

Dance

- Use symbols in abstract work (e.g. circles, straight lines, spirals, etc) to suggest shapes in which to move, or pathways.
- Go on a 'journey' through an abstract picture: identify a starting point and finishing point, with symbols in between each linked to a particular action such as jumping, turning, travelling, a gesture or stillness (*NB* these may need to be simplified, by picking out, for example, three significant features).
- Take on the stance or posture of a figure in a representational work, then add a gesture and a way of moving (travelling); repeat the sequence, aiming for fluency; maybe link in with another character (develop work in pairs or small groups).
- Pick out features in a representational or naturalistic work (e.g. tree, an animal, etc), and develop a short sequence of actions and body shapes and levels suggested by the theme (such as a way of travelling, jumping, turning, a gesture or stillness).

Example: Impressionism

Looking and responding

A group of Year 8 and 9 pupils with severe learning difficulties were shown a reproduction of Monet's 'Springtime at Giverny'. They commented freely, some noting features in the painting (house, tree, etc); one boy offered 'garden'. The pupils were invited to pretend that they were in the garden.

Developing a response

Music:
- soundscape (sound collage recorded on tape) of sounds that could go with the picture, created using the voice: individual intermittent sounds (bees, birds, etc), whilst a small group imitated the trees and grass as a continuous sound.

Drama:

- meeting teacher-in-role as the man who lived in the house in the painting (Monet!), speaking initially in French supported with Makaton signing: wearing navy beret to signify when in role, then lapsing into broken English with heavy French accent, to focus discussion through the role of Monet;
- consideration of other paintings of the garden at Giverny (favourite colours? brush strokes?), with a demonstration by 'Monet' of his favoured technique – individual pupils to imitate dabbing dots of paint.

Consolidating a response

Drama:

- pupils in role as the people whose jobs it is to keep the garden looking nice for the visitors (digging, planting flowers, weeding, cleaning out the pond, and mending the bridge, etc);
- workers meet a local official (teacher-in-role) worried about all the cars bringing people to the garden, and that more space was needed for them (e.g. making driveways through the flower beds, filling in the pond with concrete and make it in to a new car park, etc). Reactions of pupils?! Compromising interests? (e.g. landscaped car park?)

Music:

- painting exercise: practising Impressionist technique by dabbing dots of finger paint to lively, staccato French folk music.

Art:

- show pictures of Monet working up a ladder; pupils to contribute to a large group painting in the style of Monet's lily pond, using decorators' emulsioning brushes in buckets of thickly-mixed powder paint in rose pink (crimson + white), apple green (lemon yellow + cobalt blue) and sky blue (cobalt blue + white), to make short horizontal strokes, directly onto pinboard prepared with backing paper;
- individual paintings of their own house and garden (see figure 7.5 p.68), on small sized paper (A3 or A4) to contrast with the experience of working big on the collaborative piece;
- individual designs for a landscaped car park using dry materials (e.g. felt pens of differing thicknesses on A3 or A4 sized paper).

Evaluating:

Discussion: pupils to review their work, sharing it with others and talking about their pictures and any modifications they would wish to make. Using the collaborative work in the style of a Monet lily pond as backing for individual pieces, with pupils deciding where they would like their work to be displayed.

Interpreting Images

It is doubtful whether the intention of the National Curriculum Art Order is to equip society for turning out the next generation of art forgers, simply by encouraging pupils to copy the works of the great Masters! The work of other artists needs to be presented to pupils in a way that is appropriate to their stage of development, and which is relevant to:

- the pupils' mode of expression – scribbling, symbolic, analytic, etc
- the kinds of information pupils may prioritise and wish to express, reflecting their life experiences (and as extended through TV, video, cinema and books)
- the pupils' ability to control media and to realise their intentions.

Understanding and appreciating art may be linked in with topic work. For example, a theme of 'water' could prompt consideration of how different artists have depicted water, their choice of materials, tools and techniques: e.g. Hokusai (waves), Hockney (swimming pools), Turner (rough/calm sea), Monet (ponds), Macke (rain). Younger children with learning difficulties will find abstract or philosophical themes (e.g. 'destruction') difficult; themes relating to concrete objects and events common to their experience will be more accessible (e.g. 'animals', 'food', 'the home'). Younger pupils will still be able to relate to more abstract work, however – to respond to certain uses of the art elements (e.g. colour, shape, etc), even if they do not necessarily grasp the philosophical underpinning.

Children should be exposed to abstract as well as more naturalistic forms of art. Abstract art can be very liberating for children. Many forms of abstract art emphasise the importance of *process* as well as product, with the use of materials as an end in itself, so that a piece of art does not necessarily have to be *about* something (see figure 6.1 p.66). Abstract art endorses the expression of *feelings* about something or someone; a notion akin to many children's spontaneous art; bold techniques and use of strong vibrant colour in many abstract works may appeal to children on an emotional level in a way with which they may readily identify (see figure 7.1 p.66). Abstract art can overcome the notion than a piece has to look exactly like a photographic image of something or someone; this can be particularly liberating for those children frustrated with their artistic limitations (see figure 5.6 p.39). Abstract art can help foster an open-minded attitude to art, as an image may be open to many different interpretations; this may help validate the artistic expression of pupils of all abilities.

Pupils may find naturalistic work more accessible in a different way from abstract art, in that images may be more readily identifiable. These works have to be used sensitively with pupils, in order not to give the impression that they should be aspiring to quite the same level of technical expertise – certain pupils may become easily disillusioned with their artistic limitations. Nevertheless, it is important that pupils are enabled to appreciate the technical skill and degree of difficulty involved in producing certain works of art. Teachers need to lead discussion through sensitive questioning, in order to focus pupils' responses constructively. It may be that the teacher draws the pupils' attention away from appreciation of 'the whole' to the 'specific': pupils may be challenged to focus on particular use of a visual element such as patterning – can they reproduce a similar design? How has the effect of texture been created? Which materials could achieve that effect? What if different materials were used? What if a different colour was used – what would be the effect? Follow-up work – the pupils' own art-making – needs to be pitched in a way that is relevant and appropriate to their abilities, whilst illuminating their understanding of the work of naturalistic artists, and expanding their awareness of possiblities for their own artistic expression.

The previous chapters have emphasised that the teacher of art is looking to give pupils *direct experiences:* of events and objects – examined for shape, colour, form, etc – and of experimenting with tools and materials, and to bring these two explorations together. The work of other artists may be used to support, illustrate, extend, inspire and reinforce this venture, as illustrated in the following examples.

Example: abstract art

Junior age pupils with moderate learning difficulties considered the work of German Expressionist painters, such as Macke, Marck and also Klee. In particular, they looked at their use of colour and shape. They were invited to comment on whether the paintings reminded them of anything. Could they pick out anything in the pictures? They were then presented with a selection of geometric pieces of paper in different colours, which they were asked to arrange to create a 'seaside' collage in the style of Klee. They referred to secondary reference material of picture postcards and class photographs of an outing to the beach. Some pupils opted to paint their interpretation; they practised their technique in rough first to encourage attention to detail and control of edges, and mixed colours they required, before selecting which size paper they wished to use and scaling up size of brushes accordingly. Those working in collage made some trial designs and arrangements for particular images they wanted to create, before deciding on their final composition.

Example: naturalistic art

Senior age pupils with severe and moderate learning difficulties visited the Castle Museum, Norwich, and looked at watercolours by Cotman, Crome and other painters from the Norwich School. They considered historical details in the paintings, and the context in which the works were made – before the days of photography. They purchased reproduction postcards, and compared them to the originals hanging in the gallery. They compared the Norwich School landscapes of local views with photographs and postcards from modern day, and visited locations in the school minibus. They made their own sketches in pencil and/or coloured pencils, using the windows of the bus to 'frame' their drawings (see figure 6.7 p.65). Back at school, pupils attempted washes of watercolour: starting with a small amount of water, picking up paint from the dry pan using a moist brush and adding it to the water, then controlling the puddle with smooth sweeping brush strokes across good quality paper, trying to avoid streaks. They discovered how difficult the technique was! They were offered an alternative method of creating a similar effect: using aquarelles (water soluble coloured pencils). They experimented with different ways of using aquarelles: dry on dry paper, dry on wet paper (moistened with a wash of water), wet (dipping the pencil into water) on dry paper and wet on wet paper. They copied their original sketches using the aquarelles wet and/or dry, and filling in areas of colour; they then went over selected areas with a wash of water using a fine brush to achieve the translucency of a watercolour painting.

Example: objects and events

Senior pupils with severe learning difficulties looked at a selection of 'still life' reproductions by various artists, some naturalistic, others more abstract. They discussed the artists' use of different art elements (e.g. colour – whether or not it was realsitic; form – whether objects looked flat or as if you could pick them up; space – how items had been arranged, etc). They then explored a range of fruit and vegetables, looking at them closely with the aid of a magnifying glass, handling them, smelling them, etc. They decided as a group that they would like to make a 'still life' composition in the style of Cezanne. Individual pupils selected vegetables and placed them in an arrangement on a table top. They considered whether they were displayed to advantage – how had Cezanne set off his still life? They concluded that they needed to arrange them on a cloth, and to make the background less 'busy' by using a screen as a plain backdrop. The pupils sketched the vegetables using pencil, working at close hand from additional vegetables to those in the still life, to observe detail of markings, shape, etc (see figure 5.5 p.49). They experimented on rough paper with creating shades and tints, by layering oil pastels. Finally, they brought these explorations together, to produce their own interpretations on Cezanne's theme. Some pupils produced naturalistic images, others deliberately opted to use bold primary colours, more in the style of Gauguin.

Example: exploring tools, materials and techniques

Infant age pupils with severe learning difficulties were shown slides of some of Jackson Pollock's 'action paintings', projected large onto a wall. Pollock's work had entailed dribbling and trailing paint over a large canvas. The children recognised this technique, even if they did not fully understand the statement Pollock was making in respect of valuing the process rather than the product of art making. The pupils, at the 'scribbling' and 'pre/schematic/symbolic' stages of their art development, identified with such an uncomplicated technique, and the use of materials for their own sake. They made their own interpretations by squeezing ready-mixed paint straight from the bottles onto a large sheet of paper on the floor. Pupils with profound and multiple learning difficulties, at the 'scribbling' stage of their art development, also participated in a group activity. Lying over physiotherapy wedges around a large piece of paper, they swung between them a small bucket with a hole in the bottom and filled with paint suspended on string from a hook in the ceiling; this also helped to make their physiotherapy more meaningful, by providing a reason to look up, so improving their head control.

Example: cultures and traditions

Senior pupils with severe learning difficulties looked at Chinese watercolours. They were shown Chinese brushes made from goat hair, starched initially to a fine point, and how to make drawing ink from grinding an ink block on a grindstone and gradually mixing the powder with water. They experimented with creating a tonal range, by diluting the ink to varying amounts. They practised the technique of flicking the brush lightly on the paper, gripping the brush between thumb and three fingers. They were surprised and pleased at the ease with which they could achieve the effect!

Some pupils refined their technique by copying Chinese writing characters. They then each worked from a print of a Chinese watercolour (in colour), but producing their own interpretation (based on all or part of it) in a tonal range of shades of black and grey (see figure 5.4).

77

Appendix

There follows two recording sheets, for noting individual pupil progress in art. Figure A.1 (p.79) is for recording pupils' progress specifically in understanding and using the elements of art (explained in depth in chapters 3, 4, 5 and 6 of this volume of *Art for All*). Figure A.2 (p.80) is for recording pupils' overall progress in investigating and making and knowing and understanding about art (refer to chapters 2 and 7 for greater detail). On each sheet, it is possible to record pupils' achievements on six occasions – possibly once per half-term, or once a week over a half-term module. Pupils' responses may be graded 1 to 6, corresponding with the stage in the breakdown in development in the relevant area suggested in the appropriate chapter. For each aspect of art, an arbitrary, convenient, six stages of development have been identified, to indicate possible benchmarks that may be identified within a special school catering for a range of learning difficulties. As pupils with learning difficulties may 'plateau' for a long time, teachers' comments in the spaces available will be crucial for indicating *breadth* of progress by pupils.

INDIVIDUAL PROGRESS IN THE
ART ELEMENTS

Name ....

Class ....
....

begun $1 \longrightarrow 6$ acquired

	Date .... Comments, Observations, Future Priorities	Date .... Comments, Observations, Future Priorities
Ability to understand and use pattern and texture		
Ability to understand and use colour		
Ability to understand and use line and tone		
Ability to understand and use shape, form and space		

	Date .... Comments, Observations, Future Priorities	Date .... Comments, Observations, Future Priorities
Ability to understand and use pattern and texture		
Ability to understand and use colour		
Ability to understand and use line and tone		
Ability to understand and use shape, form and space		

INDIVIDUAL PROGRESS IN
MAKING AND APPRECIATING ART

Name ....

Class ....

begun 1 ⟶ 6 acquired

Ability to record responses to what has been experienced, observed and imagined

Ability to gather resources and materials to stimulate and develop ideas

Ability to explore and use two- and three-dimensional media

Ability to review and modify work

Ability to understand and apply knowledge of the work of other artists

Ability to respond to and evaluate work

Date ....
Comments, Observations, Future Priorities

Date ....
Comments, Observations, Future Priorities

Ability to record responses to what has been experienced, observed and imagined

Ability to gather resources and materials, to stimulate and develop ideas

Ability to explore and use two- and three-dimensional media

Ability to review and modify work

Ability to understand and apply knowledge of the work of other artists

Ability to respond to and evaluate work

Date ....
Comments, Observations, Future Priorities

Date ....
Comments, Observations, Future Priorities

Bibliography

Atack, S M (1980) *Art Activities for the Handicapped.* London: Souvenir Press.

Barnes, R (1987) *Teaching Art to Young Children 4–9.* London: Allen & Unwin.

Barnes, R (1989) *Art, Design and Topic Work, 8–13.* London: Routledge.

Best, D (1985) *Feeling and Reason in the Arts.* London: Allen & Unwin.

Cahill, M (1992) 'The arts and special educational needs', *Arts Education.* December, 12–15.

Coleman, A & Holder, M (1991–2) 'Textiles in the Curriculum', Art, Craft, Design and Technology, 5-part mini-series, Oct 1991–Jan 1992.

DES (1991) *Art for ages 5 to 14.* York: NCC.

DES (1992) *Art in the National Curriculum.* York: NCC.

DFE (1995) *Art in the National Curriculum.* London: HMSO.

Durbin, G, Morris, S & Wilkinson, S (1990) *A teacher's guide to Learning from Objects.* London: English Heritage.

Gentle, K (1993) *Teaching Painting in the Primary School.* London: Cassell.

Gombrich, E H (1972) *The Story of Art.* London: Phaidon Press Ltd.

Goode, S (1988) 'Spinning, Weaving and Dyeing', *Art, Craft, Design and Technology,* 5-part mini-series, Aug 1988–Jan 1989.

Greenland, M (1988–1989) 'Traditional Designs', *Art, Craft, Design and Technology* two 5-part mini-series, March–July 1988, and March–July 1989.

Gulbenkian Foundation (1982) *The Arts in Schools.* London: Calouste Gulbenkian Foundation.

Hargreaves, D H (1983) 'The teaching of art and the art of teaching: towards an alternative view of aesthetic learning', in Hammersley, M & Hargreaves, A (eds) *Curriculum Practice: some sociological case studies.* London: Falmer.

Hargreaves, D J (ed) (1989) *Children and the Arts.* Buckingham: Open University Press.

Holder, M & Coleman, A (1994) 'Creating a Design', *Art, Craft, Design and Technology.* August, pp 14–15.

ILEA (1981) *Children and clay: Clay in the Classroom.* London: ILEA Learning Materials Service.

ILEA (1987) *Learning through looking at art.* London: ILEA Gordon Teachers' Centre.

ILEA (1987) *Look Out.* London: ILEA Learning Resources Branch.

Jameson, K (1968) *Pre-School and Infant Art.* London: Studio Vista.

Jameson, K (1971) *Junior School Art.* London: Studio Vista.

Jenkins, P D (1980) *Art for the fun of it.* N J: Prentice-Hall Inc.

Kellogg, R (1969) *Analysing Children's Art.* California: Mayfield Publishing Co.

Lack, M (1992) 'Looking at Colour', *Art, Craft, Design and Technology*, 5-part mini-series, May–Aug.

Lancaster, J (ed) (1986) *Art, Craft and Design in the Primary School.* Corsham: NSEAD.

Lancaster, J (1990) *Art in the Primary School.* London: Routledge.

Lowenfeld, V & Brittan, L (1970) *Creative and Mental Growth.* New York: Macmillan.

Meizi, K (1967) *Art in the Primary School.* Oxford: Basil Blackwell.

Morgan, M (ed) (1991) *Art 4–11* Hemel Hempstead: Simon and Schuster Education.

Morgan, M (1993) *Art in Practice* Oxford: Nash Pollock.

Morris, S (1989) *A teacher's guide to Using Portraits* London: English Heritage.

Myers, B (1989) 'Looking at Pattern', *Art, Craft, Design and Technology*, 5-part mini-series, July–Dec.

NCC Arts in Schools Project (1990) *The Arts, 5–16.* Harlow: Oliver & Boyd, Longman.

OFSTED (1992) *Framework for the Inspection of Schools.* London: OFSTED.

OFSTED (1994) *Handbook for the Inspection of Schools.* London: OFSTED.

Penn, A (1994) 'Inspecting Art in the Primary School: Part two', *Art & Craft, Design & Technology.* February, pp 30–31.

Peter, M J (1987) 'A Special Presentation', *Artslink*, SCDC Arts in Schools Project, 5, 12–13.

Peter, M J (1994) *Drama For All.* London: David Fulton Publishers.

Peter, M J (1995) *Making Drama Special.* London: David Fulton Publishers.

Prokofiev, F (1994) 'The Role of an Art Therapist, part 4: Different Roles', *Art & Craft, Design & Technology.* October, pp 22–23.

Ross, M (1978) *The Creative Arts.* London: Heinemann.

Ross, M (1982) *The Development of Aesthetic Experience.* Oxford: Pergamon Press.

Ross, M (ed) (1986) *Assessment in Arts Education.* Oxford: Pergamon Press.

Ross, M (ed) (1989) *The Claims of Feeling.* London: Falmer Press.

SCDC Arts in Schools Project (1987) *A Special Collaboration.* London: SCDC.

Smith, S (1994) 'Drawing Course', in *The Art of Drawing and Painting.* London: Eaglemoss Publications Ltd.

Taylor, R (1986) *Educating for Art.* London: Longmans.

Taylor, R (1992) 'Art', in Bovair, K, Carpenter, B & Upton, G (eds) *Special Curricula Needs.* London: David Fulton Publishers Ltd.

Taylor, R & Andrews, G (1993) *The Arts in the Primary School.* London: Falmer.

Ward, D (1989) 'The arts and special needs', in Ross, M (ed) *The Claims of Feeling.* London: Falmer Press.

Whiteford, R (1991) 'A Feely Walk', *Art, Craft, Design and Technology*, Dec p3–6.

Whiteford, R (1992) 'Creating Texture', *Art, Craft, Design and Technology*, Jan p 8–9.

Witkin, R (1974) *The Intelligence of Feeling.* London: Heinemann.